Rick Bayless, JeanMarie Brownson and Deann Groen Bayless

SALSAS THAT COOK

USING CLASSIC SALSAS

TO ENLIVEN OUR

FAVORITE DISHES

PHOTOGRAPHS BY GENTL & HYERS

A FIRESIDE BOOK

Published by
Simon & Schuster

FIRESIDE
Rockefeller Center
1230 Avenue of the Americas
New York, NY 10020

Designed by Barbara M. Bachman

Set in Fairfield Med. and Triplex

Manufactured in the United States of America

3   5   7   9   10   8   6   4

Library of Congress Cataloging-in-Publication Data
Bayless, Rick.
Salsas that cook : using classic salsas to enliven our favorite dishes /
Rick Bayless, JeanMarie Brownson and Deann Groen Bayless.
p.   cm.
Includes index.
1. Salsas (Cookery). I. Brownson, JeanMarie. II. Bayless, Deann
Groen. III. Title.
TX819.S29B39   1998
641.8'14—dc21   98-42870
CIP

ISBN 0-684-85694-8

For LuAnn Bayless Tucker

ACKNOWLEDGMENTS

For years I've been more than fortunate to work with one of the country's most talented, meticulous and caring cooks, JeanMarie Brownson; one of the most intuitive, thoughtful and passionate food lovers, Deann Groen Bayless; and one of the most imaginative, insightful and experienced editors, Maria Guarnaschelli. Please accept my gratitude for your thoroughgoing input on every page of this book. Manuel Valdes, Conchita Valdes and Carlos Catá, our partners in Frontera Foods, deserve a special round of applause for their enthusiasm for this project. The creative and dedicated team at Scribner—from copy editors, art department and production personnel to Maria's assistant, Matt Thornton—were an inspiration to work with. Lisa Schumacher did the all-important work of refining and perfecting the recipes in the second round of testing, and Judy Harrold at Alltrista Corporation filled in important details about canning. Andrea Gentl, Marty Hyers, Roscoe Betsill and Helen Crowther, you've created photos that capture the true spirit of our cooking. Barbara Bachman, your design has brought beauty and useful style to a ream of text. Ross Vangalis, the cover has the flavor of Mexico and the rhythm of salsa. And Doe Coover, you're a dream of an agent.

RB

CONTENTS

5. POULTRY, MEAT AND FISH MAIN COURSES

6. DESSERTS AND DRINKS

SALSAS
THAT COOK

Introduction

I wrote this book for my sister, LuAnn. Like many of us, she works full-time, raises a family and maintains a close circle of friends. And cooks. She loves to cook, and does so very well, with a respect for tradition and a love for robust, modern flavors. But does she cook classic Mexican, the food I've given my heart to? Not as much as either one of us would like, and there is a pretty simple reason why.

Availability of ingredients for Mexican cooking is *not* the reason. There is amazing availability these days, from Seattle to Boston, San Diego to Miami. In a few short years, poblano and ancho chiles have crowded onto grocery store shelves next to Mexican oregano, *queso fresco* and good tortillas. I found everything needed to make the classic Mexican fiesta dish *mole poblano* in Muncie, Indiana, a couple of years ago. But simple availability doesn't mean we're all at the stove toasting, soaking, blending, straining and stewing the ingredients for that Mexican favorite.

The reason, I think, is that many special-occasion classics of the Mexican kitchen are time-consuming to prepare, which is typical of the cuisines of many developing countries. So lacking an invitation to a Mexican friend's fiesta, when are we going to taste this wondrous food? Most of us make one of three choices.

We have that once-a-year theme party, spending a week shopping and cooking, dressing up the house and anticipating the arrival of a crowd. Or we look for Mexican classics in restaurants, though even if we find them, rarely are they made with a grandmother's careful seasoning—which is what we strive for at my restaurants. Or, giving up hope that we're going to get those classic combinations of flavors, we decide to integrate individual Mexican ingredients into our everyday American (or Southwestern-style) dishes instead.

Any one of those choices is fine, though there's another option most of us overlook. We can utilize the classic salsas we think of solely as condiments to add complex Mexican flavor to simple dishes. True, an easily made, traditional salsa *cannot* be turned into a magnificent pot of *mole poblano*. But it *can* contribute exceptional flavor to simple Mexican dishes like creamy baked chicken, roasted pork loin with white beans or shellfish stew. These are tricks I learned from cooks in Mexico.

In a less traditional way, I also enjoy the flavors of classic salsas when glazed on roast chicken or added to mashed potatoes, or when they replace tomato sauce on pasta.

Consider the great flavors created in Chinese cooking by utilizing condiments like hoisin sauce, garlicky chile paste and a variety of soy sauces. If you think about Mexican salsas in the same way, you'll understand what the recipes in this book are all about. You'll understand that salsa can be more than a condiment. It has enough body and depth to become a baking or braising sauce; it can be stirred into favorite preparations as a flavoring ingredient. And, yes, it can simply be set out as a dip with a basket of chips or fresh vegetables.

This cookbook combines recipes for simple Mexican classics with other dishes I frequently make at home when I invite close friends and their families over for a casual meal. What I provide here is a celebration of authentic Mexican flavors that are comfortable crossing borders. Once you get these flavors into your taste memory, you'll find yourself frequently drawn to cooking in the spirit of the Mexican kitchen. These authentic flavors teach us about Mexican cooking equally as much as historical notes or details on cooking technique.

Salsas in Mexico

In Mexico, there are essentially three kinds of salsa: the chopped tomato-chile-cilantro "relish" that many of us know as "pico de gallo" or *"salsa mexicana"*; the thin, vinegary, very spicy chile sauces that are somewhat related to our Louisiana-style hot sauces (though in Mexico they have more body and flavor); and the ones that are typically made with cooked (my preference is roasted) tomatoes or tomatillos and fresh or dried chiles.

This book is about that last type of salsa. It's the most versatile of the three, using the greatest variety of chiles and providing the cook the widest range of flavors. It's also easy to make in large quantities and keeps quite well. South of the border this type of salsa is generally quite smooth, easily drizzleable and quite spicy—perfect for dashing on soft tacos or stirring into soup. North of the border, salsas that are thicker, chunkier and a little less spicy—just right for being scooped up by chips—are the choice. I've given you quite a bit of flexibility in the recipes, so you can make salsas to the consistency and spiciness you like.

How to Use This Book

First get to know some of these classic salsas. Make a small batch of two or three kinds, just to familiarize yourself with techniques, ingredients and finished flavors. You can always eat them with chips or spoon them on eggs or grilled chicken; you can spread them on sandwiches or drizzle them on simple quesadillas.

Next read through the rest of the recipes and decide what appeals. If you like the smoky Chipotle-Cascabel Salsa, you'll probably want to try it on the Chile-Glazed Roast Chicken and in Chipotle Mashed Potatoes. If brunch is a favorite time to cook for family and friends, look at the recipe for the Savory Brunch Bread Pudding.

Now you'll have to decide how much to make, and that's where we can help. We've designed the salsa recipes to be uncomplicated to make in large quantities. They keep well. They can even be preserved by freezing or canning. Each salsa recipe gives quantities for a small amount (what I call a "tasting" amount); a medium amount (enough for one recipe, with leftovers to put out as a condiment); and a large amount. The large amount provides the right quantity for three or four dishes, and since the salsas can be frozen, canned or simply stored in the refrigerator for up to five days, making the large batch has appeal—large batches take almost no more time than small ones.

And when tomatoes, tomatillos and chiles are in season in your garden or at the farmers' market or when you have some time to spend in the kitchen, can a large (or double or triple batch), and you'll have a secret weapon (or very special gift) at the ready for simple, wonderful meals.

SALSAS

ROASTED JALAPEÑO-TOMATO SALSA WITH FRESH CILANTRO
• ROASTED POBLANO-TOMATO SALSA WITH FRESH THYME •
ROASTED TOMATILLO SALSA WITH SERRANOS, ROASTED
ONIONS AND CILANTRO • MELLOW RED CHILE SALSA WITH
SWEET GARLIC AND ROASTED TOMATOES • ROASTY RED
GUAJILLO SALSA WITH TANGY TOMATILLOS AND SWEET
GARLIC • CHIPOTLE-CASCABEL SALSA WITH ROASTED
TOMATOES AND TOMATILLOS

Here are the basics—six salsas that keep well, present a wide range of flavors, and offer beautifully balanced ingredients using techniques that bring out their best.

The first two salsas are based on fresh chiles and roasted tomatoes, one specifically developed for small fresh chiles (we've made it here with jalapeños) and one for large fresh chiles (here poblanos).

- **Roasted Jalapeño-Tomato Salsa** with fresh cilantro—The classic balance of sweet-roasted tomato, green chile and cilantro teaches us why this salsa is a versatile player, as good dolloped on tacos as it is simmered in rice or beef stew.
- **Roasted Poblano-Tomato Salsa** with fresh thyme—This salsa celebrates complex roasted green chile flavor sweetened with roasted tomato. It easily works its way into baked fish dishes and marinades.

Then there's the green salsa made from tomatillos, which you can think of (in terms of proportions and techniques) as a green version of the roasted tomato-jalapeño salsa—tomatillos replacing tomatoes, serranos replacing jalapeños.

✳ **Roasted Tomatillo Salsa** with serranos, roasted onions and cilantro—The lively tanginess of this salsa is underscored by sweet roastiness, bringing to mind seared fish, roasted pork and anything rich—from avocados to scalloped potatoes.

Lastly, there are three salsas based on dried chiles. You'll notice that the smaller and hotter the dried chile, the less you use. All three rely on tomatoes or tomatillos (or a combination of the two) to carry the earthy punch of the dried chiles.

✳ **Mellow Red Chile Salsa** with sweet garlic and roasted tomatoes—The earthy but mild gentleness of this red chile salsa makes it perfect as a replacement for tomato sauce to coat pasta, sauce eggs or marinate chicken for roasting or grilling.

✳ **Roasty Red Guajillo Salsa** with tangy tomatillos and sweet garlic—The roasty undertones of this salsa are enlivened with the beguiling straightforward dried chile flavor of guajillos, creating a delicious match for lamb, beef or the unique flavor of shellfish.

✳ **Chipotle-Cascabel Salsa** with roasted tomatoes and tomatillos—The perfect balance of sweetness, smokiness, brightness and complex intensity gives this salsa a compelling flavor that is ideal on practically everything but breakfast cereal.

Once you've come to know the salsas, you can feel free to play around with them, perhaps replacing chiles from your garden, farmers' market or grocery store for the poblanos, jalapeños and serranos. Just remember to replace size for size, more or less. When you wander the aisles of Mexican groceries, gourmet stores and well-stocked supermarkets, keep your eye out for dried chiles. Buy what you can find, and try them out in the three dried chile salsas, again replacing size for size as best you can.

The Techniques and Equipment

You'll notice that we've roasted or toasted most all the ingredients in these salsas. First, cooking the ingredients is what gives them a longer life—in the refrigerator, freezer or the canning jar. Second, roasting (as opposed to boiling) deepens and sweetens the flavors of the vegetables and chiles, infusing the finished salsa with a wonderful complexity.

In many traditional Mexican households, the roasting would be done directly on a *comal* (an earthenware or metal griddle—the same piece of kitchen equipment used for griddle-baked tortillas) or in *very* traditional households directly in live coals (mostly used for whole heads of garlic and whole onions). I've translated the griddle-roasting to the broiler simply because the broiler requires less attention and cooks more evenly. Some cooks like to line the baking sheet with heavy-duty foil to make collection of juices and cleanup easier.

If you want to try the traditional Mexican griddle-roasting technique, lay your tomatoes or tomatillos directly on a medium-hot, ungreased griddle set over medium heat. Then griddle-roast, turning occasionally, until the tomatoes or tomatillos are very soft and blackened in spots. Garlic can be cooked this way too, but leave it in its papery skin and peel after roasting. As for roasting onions on a griddle, I like to have them in slices so that I can roast them on one side, then flip them over and roast them on the other. I prefer to griddle-roast everything except garlic on a piece of foil to make cleanup easier (tomatoes, tomatillos and onions tend to stick). If you like smoky flavor, you can roast the onion and garlic on a perforated grill pan over a moderately low charcoal fire for about the same amount of time.

Though dried chiles can be toasted under a broiler, the intensity of the heat is a little too high. I still get the best results from the old-fashioned griddle-toasting unless, of course, I'm oil-toasting as in the Roasty Red Guajillo Salsa. Oil-toasting gives a more intense toasty flavor with a crisp-fried edge to it.

Though for millennia Mexican cooks have used lava-rock *molcajetes* and *metates* to work vegetables and chiles into a salsa consistency, a food processor and blender are easier choices for most modern cooks. The **food processor** is extremely efficient for chopping relatively dry mixtures of vegetables and for *coarsely* pureeing tomatoes and tomatillos. The **blender** likes saucy mixtures. In fact, chopping vegetables in a blender can seem tedious because the vegetables must be chopped in small amounts and constantly scraped off the sides of the container. Because of the blender's shape and the fact that the blades go much faster than those of a food processor, it works excellently, even better than a food processor, when making saucy salsas that contain the tough-skinned *dried* chiles. If you have one piece of equipment but not the other, you can still make great salsa—you'll just have to pay attention to the strengths or weaknesses of your appliance. If you're working with large quantities, keep in mind that not all the ingredients will fit in either piece of equipment; you'll need to work in batches.

Choosing Ingredients

Tomatoes and Tomatillos: These two ingredients provide the background against which the flavors of chiles stand out.

Tomatoes are nearly always called for **fresh and ripe** in this book, and in most cases I suggest using the plum variety because it will give you a more homogeneous consistency, making the salsa more versatile for cooking. Besides, plum tomatoes often show up riper than round tomatoes in the groceries year round, and even if they're not as ripe as you'd like, a few days on the counter will result in decent flavor and color. **Using canned tomatoes:** I use canned tomatoes when ripe tomatoes are not available, even though I miss all the roasted flavor. Substitute a *drained* 28-ounce can of plum tomatoes for 1½ pounds of fresh tomatoes and skip the roasting step.

Tomatillos, like tomatoes, are always called for **fresh** in these recipes. They are quite easily available year round, they keep well (weeks in the refrigerator), and they offer almost none of the ripeness problems that tomatoes do. **Using canned tomatillos:** In a word, **don't.** They are soft and watery, they take on the flavor of the can, and there's usually a briny flavor in the canning juices. Also, if you choose canned tomatillos, you'll really miss the sweetness that roasting imparts to these tart little fruits.

Fresh Chiles: Let's keep matters simple: "Chiles" and "peppers" are words that describe the same thing, nomenclature being, perhaps, the most difficult aspect of working with these native American fruits. Fresh chiles are nearly always available throughout the United States, especially in well-stocked grocery stores and Mexican markets. If you live in the West or Southwest, you'll likely notice less availability of the fresh, large, dark green somewhat triangular **poblano chile** (poblanos may be called "fresh pasillas" on the West Coast) than of the larger, lighter-skinned, more tubular-shaped **Anaheim (long green) chile.** But both can be found most everywhere in the country.

The smaller fresh **jalapeños** (stubby 1½-inch medium green chiles with a noticeable shoulder that slopes down to a blunt point) and **serranos** (smaller, lighter green and more bullet shaped than jalapeños) are widely available; if neither is in your market, I've given a number of alternatives, including **habaneros.**

Green chiles or red ones? Green chiles have the punchiest, "greenest" flavor, which most agree combines well with roasted tomatoes and tomatillos. Red chiles, with their softer and sweeter flesh, are preferred by some cooks.

Always choose the most unblemished fresh chiles with the tautest skins and firmest flesh; they're the freshest. Fresh chiles will keep for a week or more in your refrigerator, loosely wrapped.

Dried Chiles: Explaining these is a bit more complicated, because there's even more variation in the nomenclature than with fresh chiles and they're not as readily available in some areas. Of the larger dried ones, **New Mexico chiles** (the dark-cranberry-colored, smooth-skinned chiles that are 6 to 7 inches long and usually marked mild or hot) may be the most available nationally (they are the most widely grown in the United States since they go into a lot of paprika). More popular in Chicago are dried **guajillo chiles** (they resemble the New Mexicos but are typically shorter and nearly always medium-hot to hot).

With respect to the smaller dried chiles, I think it's safe to say that we want flavor along with the tongue tingling we've associated with cayenne and red pepper flakes. So it's no wonder that **chipotle chiles** are our favorites: These dried jalapeños are smoky and pack a punch that brings a sense of euphoria rather than desperation. In Mexico, there are two kinds: small (1- to 1½-inch), dark cranberry red, wrinkle-skinned *chiles chipotles colorados,* often sold in the United States as *moritas,* and the larger (2- to 2½-inch), tan, wrinkle-skinned *chiles chipotles mecos.* If you can't find dried, look for a rehydrated canned version labeled *chiles chipotles en adobo;* they're usually made from the *chipotles colorados* packed in a vinegary tomato sauce (*adobo*). I find them easy to work with, since no toasting and soaking is necessary.

Cascabel chiles, though available in a great number of Mexican markets, haven't crossed over to the grocery stores in most places. These are dark-cranberry-colored chiles with a hint of tan or brown; they are spherical in shape (about 1 inch in diameter) with a smooth, somewhat brittle skin that obviously has little flesh beneath it. Their flavor is wonderfully complex and nutty with a medium amount of heat.

When you can, choose chiles that are whole, vibrantly and evenly colored (indicating recent harvesting and drying and no larval infestation) and supple (which means they are picked healthy and treated well during harvesting and drying). Store dried chiles well wrapped in the freezer or in airtight containers in a cool, dry place.

Onions and Garlic: As you'll notice, onions and garlic run like a warp through these marvelously diverse salsas. They provide sweetness, texture and, in some cases, the strength to support even bolder flavors. In every recipe they're roasted, which minimizes their aggressiveness and maximizes their sweetness. Roasting also ensures that their flavor won't take over salsas that are stored in the refrigerator or canning jars.

For classic Mexican flavor and the "cleanest" taste, we've mostly called for **white onions.** Their bright flavor blends much better with chiles, tomatoes and cilantro than the muted flavor of yellow onions. Though the type of garlic you use is less important in these recipes, just be aware that varieties with small cloves are often more pungent.

Fresh Herbs: The most common fresh herb used in these recipes is **cilantro** (occasionally, though less and less, called fresh coriander or Chinese parsley). It is very widely available. I refrigerate it in a jar or mug with a small amount of water in the bottom and covered with a plastic bag; it'll hold up for several days quite nicely. In two salsa recipes we've called for **fresh thyme,** which is very easy to grow and, thankfully, readily available in well-stocked grocery stores. If you simply can't find any, replace every teaspoon of it with a scant ½ teaspoon of dried.

Advance Preparation

Because most all of the ingredients in the following six recipes are cooked in some fashion, these salsas can be kept in the refrigerator for several days—preferably not more than five—without much change in flavor or texture.

For the same reason, these salsas do well under the strain that canning puts on a recipe, which is particularly useful in times of bounty from your garden or farmers' market. If you wish to can these salsas after making them, heat them in a saucepan to 185 degrees (use an instant-read thermometer) for several minutes before you pack them into hot well-washed canning jars to within ¼ inch of the top. Seal the jars with new vacuum-sealing lids and then follow the instructions from a manufacturer of home canning jars for the proper processing method and time. After processing and cooling, I check to make sure each lid has sealed tightly—the center will look slightly concave and not pop up and down when pressed. Because my salsa recipes don't include a lot of vinegar, I use any that I have canned at home within a month or so.

And the freezer? Use it, I say, but don't leave the salsa there for more than 3 or 4 months, and be ready for a different texture when defrosted. It'll likely look a little watery and broken (especially salsa with tomatillos in it), but this problem can usually be remedied by a thorough beating with a whisk or fork.

Using Bottled Salsas

Though there are a mind-boggling number of salsas on the market, most are of the tangy tomatoey kind, perhaps with a little green chile and cilantro added. Most of these salsas will work adequately for the recipes in this book that call for Roasted Jalapeño-Tomato Salsa or Roasted Poblano-Tomato Salsa. You'll note that most bottled salsas on the market contain considerably more vinegar than we call for, which will definitely affect the taste of the finished dish.

Few manufacturers, however, have delved into the rich variety of Mexican salsas. Under the brand name Frontera, we produce a line of salsas made from roasted fresh ingredients that mirrors the complexity of the recipes we've included here. Since the names of the salsas in this chapter are very similar to our bottled line, feel free, when time or energy is short, to measure out an equivalent amount of the bottled salsa wherever the homemade is called for. (See Sources, page 122, for more information.) We have tested all our recipes with homemade and our bottled salsa and can enthusiastically endorse both.

Roasted Jalapeño-Tomato Salsa with fresh cilantro

· · · · ·

This is our salsa closest to the classic home-style Mexican salsa de molcajete *that's made from roasted garlic and chiles pounded in a lava-rock mortar (molcajete) with roasted tomatoes. Even though we've updated the equipment for the modern American kitchen, that perfect blend of sweetness (roasted garlic and tomatoes) and raciness (roasted jalapeños) is what you'll spoon out. The final addition of fresh cilantro and a drizzle of vinegar focuses the whole experience: This is just what most Americans wish they were getting when they open a jar with that ubiquitous "salsa" label. Made with plum tomatoes, your salsa will have a more homogeneous texture—just right for using the salsa as an ingredient in other dishes. Because round tomatoes give a looser texture, choose them when you want a condiment to set on the table.*

	FOR 2½ CUPS	FOR 5 CUPS	FOR 7½ CUPS
Ripe tomatoes, preferably plum	1½ pounds (about 10 medium plum)	3 pounds (about 20 medium plum)	4½ pounds (about 30 medium plum)
Fresh jalapeño chiles, stemmed	2 to 3 (1 to 1½ ounces)	4 to 6 (2 to 3 ounces)	6 to 9 (3 to 4½ ounces)
White onion, sliced ¼ inch thick	½ small (2 ounces)	1 small (4 ounces)	1 medium (6 ounces)
Garlic cloves, peeled	4	8	12
Water	about ¼ cup	about ½ cup	about ¾ cup

Chopped fresh cilantro, loosely packed	⅓ cup	⅔ cup	1 cup
Salt	1 generous teaspoon	2 generous teaspoons	1 generous tablespoon
Cider vinegar	1½ teaspoons	1 tablespoon	1½ tablespoons

OTHER FRESH CHILE POSSIBILITIES:

Habanero (orange or green), serrano, Santa Fe, Fresno, fresh pequín, Hungarian wax, fresh arbol, cayenne, Tabasco, as well as most small hot fresh chiles.

1. Heat the broiler. Lay the whole tomatoes and jalapeños out on a broiler pan or baking sheet. Set the pan 4 inches below the broiler and broil for about 6 minutes, until darkly roasted—even blackened in spots—on one side (the tomato skins will split and curl in places). With a pair of tongs, flip over the tomatoes and chiles and roast the other side for another 6 minutes or so. The goal is not simply to char the tomatoes and chiles but to cook them through while developing nice roasty flavors. Set aside to cool.

2. Turn the oven down to 425 degrees. Separate the onions into rings. On a similar pan or baking sheet, combine the onion and garlic. Roast in the oven, stirring carefully every couple of minutes, until the onions are beautifully browned and wilted (even have a touch of char on some of the edges) and the garlic is soft and browned in spots, about 15 minutes total. Cool to room temperature.

3. For a little less rustic texture or if you're canning the salsa, pull off the peels from the cooled tomatoes and cut out the "cores" where the stems were attached, working over your baking sheet so as not to waste any juices. In a food processor, pulse the jalapeños (no need to peel or seed them) with the onion and garlic until moderately finely chopped, scraping everything down with a spatula as needed to keep it all moving around. Scoop into a big bowl. Without washing the processor, coarsely puree the tomatoes—with all the juice

that has accumulated around them—and add them to the bowl. Stir in enough water to give the salsa an easily spoonable consistency. Stir in the cilantro.

4. Taste and season with salt and vinegar, remembering that this condiment should be a little feisty in its seasoning. **If you're planning to use your salsa right away,** simply pour it into a bowl and it's ready, or refrigerate it covered and use within 5 days. **If you're canning or freezing the salsa,** please see page 21.

VARIATION:
ROASTED HABANERO-TOMATO SALSA:

To make this very spicy, distinctively flavored salsa, replace the jalapeños with 2/4/6 stemmed habanero chiles (here I prefer the fruitier flavor of the orange habaneros to the less ripe—even grassy—flavor of the greens).

DISHES YOU CAN MAKE WITH THIS SALSA:

Salsa-Baked Goat Cheese (page 41), Classic Red Tomato Rice (page 62), Breakfast Enchiladas (page 68), Today's Macaroni and Cheese (page 72), Toasty *Fideos* (Vermicelli) with Roasted Tomato, Black Beans and Chard (page 74), Spicy Jalapeño Beef Tips (page 97). Seared Sea Scallops with Jalapeño Cream (page 106)

Roasted Poblano-Tomato Salsa with fresh thyme

Though this salsa is a close cousin of the Roasted Jalapeño-Tomato Salsa, its flavors are more mellow (more roasted chiles but ones with a richer, less bitey flavor), and its consistency is saucier (you'll notice the addition of tomato puree). Red onion adds more sweetness than white, and the touch of thyme adds a gentle complexity that you'd never get with cilantro alone. The result: a salsa that easily doubles as a sauce. Use the pulpier plum tomatoes rather than round ones for the sauciest consistency.

	FOR 3 CUPS	FOR 6 CUPS	FOR 9 CUPS
Ripe tomatoes preferably plum	1 pound (6 to 7 medium plum)	2 pounds (about 14 medium plum)	3 pounds (about 20 medium plum)
Fresh poblano chiles	2 medium (5 ounces)	4 medium (10 ounces)	6 medium (15 ounces)
Red onion, sliced ¼ inch thick	½ small (2 ounces)	1 small (4 ounces)	1 medium (6 ounces)
Garlic cloves, peeled	4	8	12
Good-quality canned tomato puree	½ cup	1 cup	1½ cups
Water	about ½ cup	about 1 cup	about 1½ cups
Chopped fresh cilantro, loosely packed	2 tablespoons	¼ cup	6 tablespoons
Chopped fresh thyme	2 teaspoons	4 teaspoons	2 tablespoons
Salt	2 teaspoons	4 teaspoons	2 tablespoons

1. Heat the broiler. Lay the whole tomatoes and poblanos out on a broiler pan or baking sheet. Set the pan as close to the broiler as your oven allows and broil for about 6 minutes, until darkly roasted and splotchy black on one side. With a pair of tongs, flip over the tomatoes and chiles and roast the other side. The poblanos may be completely blistered and blackened before the tomatoes are—remove them as soon as they are done.

2. Turn the oven down to 425 degrees. Separate the onion into rings. On a similar pan or baking sheet, mix together the onion and garlic. Roast in the oven, stirring every few minutes, until the onions are richly browned (they'll look soft, even have a touch of char on some of the edges) and the garlic feels soft and is browned in spots, about 15 minutes total. Cool to room temperature.

3. If you don't like a rustic-textured salsa or if you're canning the salsa, pull the peels from the cooled tomatoes and cut out the "cores" where the stems were attached, working over your baking sheet to collect the juices. Pull the peels off the chiles, then pull out the stem and the seed pod. Tear the poblanos open and rinse quickly to remove all the stray seeds. Chop into ¼-inch pieces and place in a large bowl.

4. In a food processor, pulse the onion and garlic until moderately finely chopped; scrape down to ensure even chopping. Scoop into the bowl with the chopped poblanos. Without washing the processor, coarsely puree the tomatoes with their juice, then add them to the bowl. Stir in the tomato sauce puree and enough water to give the salsa a rather light, saucy consistency. Stir in the cilantro and thyme.

5. Taste the salsa and season it with salt, pushing the flavors toward the upper levels. **If you're planning to use your salsa right away,** simply pour it into a bowl and it's ready, or refrigerate it covered and use within 5 days. **If you're canning or freezing the salsa,** please see page 21.

OTHER FRESH CHILE POSSIBILITIES:

Anaheim (long green), large Hungarian wax, chilaca, cubanelle.

DISHES YOU CAN MAKE WITH THIS SALSA:

Crispy *Masa* Boat Snacks (page 46), Poblano-Roasted Vegetable Salad (page 57), Today's Macaroni and Cheese (page 72), Soft Tacos of Grilled Chicken Breast (page 86), Grilled-and-Glazed Pork Tenderloin (page 100), Poblano-Baked Fish Fillets (page 110)

Roasted Tomatillo Salsa with serranos, roasted onions and cilantro

The native American husk-covered "tomato" known as tomatillo (it's a relative of the vining little ground cherry that grows wild all over the United States) is tang personified. But when you roast it, you mellow its precocious flavor into zesty richness. Serrano chiles deliver a fresh-green bite, while cilantro adds just the right herbal punch. If you've shied away from green salsas, finding them acrid and briny, try this very fresh tasting roasted tomatillo salsa and you'll be won back.

	FOR 2 CUPS	FOR 4 CUPS	FOR 6 CUPS
Tomatillos, husked and rinsed	1 pound (7 medium)	2 pounds (about 14 medium)	3 pounds (21 medium)
Fresh serrano chiles, stemmed	4 to 5 (¾ to 1 ounce)	8 to 10 (1½ to 2 ounces)	12 to 15 (2½ to 3 ounces)
White onion, sliced ¼ inch thick	1 small (4 ounces)	1 large (8 ounces)	2 medium (12 ounces)
Garlic cloves, peeled	3	6	9
Water	about ½ cup	about 1 cup	about 1½ cups
Chopped fresh cilantro, loosely packed	⅓ cup	⅔ cup	1 cup
Salt	about 1 teaspoon	about 2 teaspoons	about 1 tablespoon
Sugar (optional)	1 teaspoon	2 teaspoons	1 tablespoon

1. Heat the broiler. Lay the whole tomatillos and serranos on a broiler pan or baking sheet. Set the pan 4 inches below the broiler and let roast until the tomatillos are softened and splotchy black in places (the skins will split), about 5 minutes; your goal is to cook the tomatillos *through* while they roast, which means they'll change from light bright green to olive green on the top side. With a pair of tongs, flip over the tomatillos and chiles and roast the other side for another 4 to 5 minutes or so. Set aside to cool.

2. Turn the oven down to 425 degrees. Separate the onion into rings and, on a similar pan or baking sheet, combine them with the garlic. Place in the oven. Stir carefully every couple of minutes, until the onions are beautifully browned. (They're going to look wilted and translucent, even have a touch of char on some of the edges.) The garlic should feel soft and be browned in spots. The total roasting time will be about 15 minutes. Cool to room temperature.

3. In a food processor, place the onion-garlic mixture and the serranos, and pulse until moderately finely chopped, scraping everything down with a spatula as needed to keep it all moving. Scoop the mixture into a large bowl. Without washing the processor, coarsely puree the tomatillos with their juice—no need to peel off their darkened skin or cut out their cores. Stir them into the chiles. Stir in enough water to give the salsa an easily spoonable consistency. Stir in the cilantro.

4. Taste and season highly with salt. Taste again and, if you like, add just enough sugar to take the edge off the bright tanginess of the tomatillos. **If you're planning to use your salsa right away,** simply pour it into a bowl and it's ready, or refrigerate it covered and use within 5 days. **If you're canning or freezing the salsa,** please see page 21.

OTHER FRESH CHILE POSSIBILITIES:

Jalapeño, Santa Fe, Fresno, fresh pequín, finger hots, Hungarian wax.

DISHES YOU CAN MAKE WITH THIS SALSA:

Tangy Green Guacamole (page 40), Emerald Corn Chowder (page 53), Tangy Lentil Salad (page 58), Scalloped Potatoes (page 64), Open-Face Chorizo-Potato Omelet (page 67), Tomatillo-Baked Chicken Breasts (page 85), Tomatillo-Braised Pork Loin (page 98), Green Chile Crab Cakes (page 107)

Mellow Red Chile Salsa with sweet garlic and roasted tomatoes

As you progress from fresh chiles to dried ones, the flavors deepen and concentrate; they become more robust and complex. These flavors are the genius of the Mexican kitchen.

Dried New Mexico chiles, whether mild or hot, offer the lightest, easiest of the dried chile flavors. So start with this salsa if you're new to this genre. The dried-chile earthiness of the New Mexicos—dressed up with a good portion of sweet roasted tomatoes and garlic, perfumed with a little Mexican oregano, jazzed up with a dash of vinegar—is offered here at its most perfectly mellow best.

	FOR 2½ CUPS	FOR 5 CUPS	FOR 7½ CUPS
Dried New Mexico chiles	4 (1⅓ ounces)	8 (2⅔ ounces)	12 (4 ounces)
Ripe tomatoes, preferably plum	½ pound (3 medium plum)	1 pound (6 to 7 medium plum)	1½ pounds (about 10 medium plum)
White onion, sliced ¼ inch thick	½ small (2 ounces)	1 small (4 ounces)	1 medium (6 ounces)
Garlic cloves, peeled	½ head	1 head	1½ heads
Dried oregano, preferably Mexican	¼ teaspoon	½ teaspoon	¾ teaspoon
Cider vinegar	1½ tablespoons	3 tablespoons	4½ tablespoons
Water	about ½ cup	about 1 cup	about 1½ cups
Salt	1½ teaspoons	1 tablespoon	1½ tablespoons
Sugar (optional)	¼ teaspoon	½ teaspoon	¾ teaspoon

1. Heat the broiler. Pull the stems off the dried chiles, tear them open and shake out the seeds (if you prefer a salsa with a more refined texture, be sure to remove all the seeds). Place in a bowl, cover with hot tap water and lay a plate on top to keep them submerged.

2. Lay the whole tomatoes on a broiler pan or baking sheet. Set as close to the broiler as your oven allows and broil for about 6 minutes, until darkly roasted and blackened in spots—the tomato skins will split and curl. With a pair of tongs, flip over the tomatoes and roast them for another 6 minutes or so, until they are soft and splotched with dark spots. Set aside to cool.

3. Turn the oven down to 425 degrees. Separate the onion into rings and, on a pan or baking sheet, combine it with the garlic. Set in the oven. Stir carefully every few minutes, until the onions are soft and beautifully roasted (don't worry if some of the edges char) and the garlic is soft and browned in spots, about 15 minutes total.

4. If you're not inclined toward rustic textures in your salsa or if you're canning the salsa, pull off the peels from the cooled tomatoes and cut out the "cores" where the stems were attached; catch the flavorful juices on the baking sheet as you work, so as not to waste any of them. By now the chiles should be soft (to catch them at the perfect stage of rehydration—before they've lost much flavor into the water—soak them no longer than 30 minutes); drain. In a blender or food processor, combine the drained chiles with the tomatoes and their juice. Process to a fairly smooth puree—chile skins are tough, so you want to make sure they are chopped up enough. Scrape two-thirds of the puree into a large bowl. Roughly chop the onion and garlic, then add them to the blender containing the rest of the chile-tomato mixture. Pulse repeatedly until all is moderately finely chopped. Scrape down the sides from time to time to keep everything

OTHER DRIED CHILE POSSIBILITIES:

Guajillo, pulla.

**DISHES YOU CAN
MAKE WITH THIS
SALSA:**

Sweet-and-Spicy
Chilied Pork Empanadas
(page 44), Great Tor-
tilla Soup (page 52),
Red Chile-Jícama Salad
(page 56), Racy Egg-
plant Omelets (page
66), Red Chile Pasta
(page 71), Seared Red-
Chile Enchiladas (page
78), Burnished Cornish
Hens (page 88), Robust
Beef Brisket (page 92),
Red Chile Rice with
Shrimp and Bacon
(page 105), Red-Glazed
Whole Fish (page 108)

moving evenly; if the mixture just won't move through the blades, add a little water to loosen it up. Scrape the puree into the bowl. Stir in the oregano and vinegar, then add enough water to give this salsa a light consistency.

5. Taste and season generously with salt—this is a condiment, remember. Taste again and add a little sugar if you think it's necessary to balance any lingering bitterness in the chiles. **If you're planning to use your salsa right away,** simply pour it into a bowl and it's ready, or refrigerate it covered and use within 5 days. **If you're canning or freezing the salsa,** please see page 21.

Perfectly roasted fresh jalapeño and poblano chiles; tomatoes and tomatillos;
jars of homemade salsas; roasted onions and garlic

Fresh and dried chiles. *From left to right:* *(bottom)* Anaheim (long green), serrano;
(second row) dried chipotle (morita), poblano, dried New Mexico; *(third row)* dried
cascabel *(in bowl)*, habanero, jalapeño; *(top)* dried guajillo

Tiny Tostadas of Smoky Chicken *Tinga* (page 43); Honest-to-Goodness
Margaritas for a Crowd (page 120)

Sweet-and-Spicy Chilied Pork Empanadas (page 44)

Shrimp in Red Escabeche (page 48)

Emerald Corn Chowder with roasted
tomatillos and poblano (page 53)

Shrimp *Salpicón* Salad with potatoes,
avocados and chipotle (page 54)

Red Chile-Jícama Salad with orange
and red onion (page 56)

Roasty Red Guajillo Salsa with tangy tomatillos and sweet garlic

In this salsa resides magic—deeply traditional, soulful, rich red-chile magic. It's worlds away from roasted tomatoes and jalapeños (which is what most of us Americans think of as "salsa"), and it's on the other side of town from the more familiar red-chile mellowness of the preceding recipe. This is salsa with the robust roastiness of oil-toasted dried guajillos (they're bright in flavor, a little bitey) combined with sweet roasted garlic and onions, plus the zestiness of tomatillos. All in all, a most satisfying, most versatile, most Mexican-tasting salsa.

	FOR 2 CUPS	FOR 4 CUPS	FOR 6 CUPS
Vegetable oil	¼ inch depth	¼ inch depth	¼ inch depth
Dried guajillo chiles	4 (1 ounce)	8 (2 ounces)	12 (3 ounces)
Tomatillos, husked and rinsed	1 pound (about 13 medium)	2 pounds (about 26 medium)	3 pounds (about 40 medium)
White onion, sliced ¼ inch thick	½ small (2 ounces)	1 small (4 ounces)	1 medium (6 ounces)
Garlic cloves, peeled	4	8	12
Water	about ¾ cup	about 1½ cups	about 2¼ cups
Salt	1½ teaspoons	1 tablespoon	1½ tablespoons
Sugar (optional)	½ teaspoon	1 teaspoon	1½ teaspoons

1. Heat the broiler. Pour the oil to a ¼-inch depth in a small skillet and set over medium heat. Pull the stems off the chiles, then tear them open and shake out the seeds. By this time the oil should be hot. Lay a chile in it: the oil should be hot enough to bubble nicely—not slowly, not fiercely. Use a pair of tongs to turn it over several times as it toasts and changes color on the inside from dark cranberry red to a reddish tan; the toasting of each chile should take 15 to 20 seconds. Thoroughly toasting the chiles is essential for good flavor, but toasting them too long will result in bitterness in the finished salsa. Drain the toasted chiles on paper towels; they will crisp completely as they cool.

2. Lay the whole tomatillos on a broiler pan or baking sheet. Set the pan 4 inches below the broiler and let roast until the tomatillos are softened and splotchy black in places (the skins will split), about 5 minutes; you are cooking the tomatillos *through* while they roast, which means they will change from light green to olive green in the process. With a pair of tongs, flip over the tomatillos and roast the other side for another 4 to 5 minutes or so. Set aside to cool. There is no need to peel off their darkened skins or cut out their cores.

3. Turn the oven down to 425 degrees. On a similar pan or baking sheet, combine the onion (separated into rings) and the garlic. Set in the oven. Stir every couple of minutes, being careful to stir everything around, until the onions are deeply golden—they'll look somewhat wilted with a touch of char on some of the edges. The garlic should feel soft and be browned in spots. Total roasting time will be about 15 minutes. Cool to room temperature.

4. In a blender or food processor, combine the tomatillos with their juice and the dry toasted chiles. Process to quite a smooth puree. Scrape two-thirds of the puree into a large bowl. On a cutting board, roughly chop the onion and gar-

lic. Add them to the blender still containing the rest of the chile mixture. Pulse repeatedly until all is moderately finely chopped. Scrape down the blender sides periodically to keep the mixture evenly moving through the blades; add a little water if needed to loosen everything up and keep it moving. Scrape into the bowl. Stir in enough water to give this salsa a light consistency.

5. Taste and season highly with salt, remembering that condiments are more boldly seasoned than other foods. Now taste again and add a little sugar to balance any astringency from the chiles. **If you're planning to use your salsa right away,** simply pour it into a bowl and it's ready, or refrigerate it covered and use within 5 days. **If you're canning or freezing the salsa,** please see page 21.

DISHES YOU CAN MAKE WITH THIS SALSA:

Shrimp in Red Escabeche (page 48), Guajillo Grilled Vegetables (page 60), *Chilaquiles* (Tortilla Casserole) with spinach, zucchini and aged cheese (page 76), Slow-Grilled Turkey Breast (or Lamb Leg) with Mediterranean Salsa (page 90), Chorizo and Black Bean Chili (page 96), Guajillo-Spiked Shellfish Soup (page 104)

Chipotle-Cascabel Salsa with roasted tomatoes and tomatillos

• • • • • •

This is salsa at its complex best: smoky fire from those beloved little chipotles (smoke-dried jalapeños), nutty intricacy from dried cascabels, sweetness from roasted tomatoes and garlic, zestiness from tomatillos. There are so many wonderful things going on here, taste-wise, that you'll feel compelled to try it again and again. The dried chipotles are easier to find than the dried cascabel chiles; if cascabels are not available, make a very good salsa with all chipotles. When you can only find canned chipotles (I'm referring here to the widely available, very popular ones packed in the vinegary tomato sauce called adobo—it'll say that on the can), you can substitute those for one or both of the dried chiles; skip the toasting and soaking in the first step.

	FOR 2 CUPS	FOR 4 CUPS	FOR 6 CUPS
Dried chipotle chiles	3 (⅓ ounce)	6 (⅔ ounce)	9 (1 ounce)
Dried round cascabel chiles	3 (⅓ ounce)	6 (⅔ ounce)	9 (1 ounce)
Tomatillos, husked and rinsed	½ pound (6 to 7 medium)	1 pound (about 13 medium)	1½ pounds (about 20 medium)
Ripe tomatoes, preferably plum	½ pound (3 medium plum)	1 pound (6 to 7 medium plum)	1½ pounds (about 10 medium plum)
Garlic cloves, peeled	6	12	18
White onion, sliced ¼ inch thick	1 large (½ pound)	2 large (1 pound)	3 large (1½ pounds)

Chopped fresh thyme	1½ teaspoons	1 tablespoon	1½ tablespoons
Water	about ½ cup	about 1 cup	about 1½ cups
Salt	1 generous teaspoon	2 generous teaspoons	1 generous tablespoon
Sugar (optional)	½ teaspoon	1 teaspoon	1½ teaspoons

1. Heat the broiler and set a heavy skillet over medium heat. Break the stems off the chiles, scoop them into the heating pan and stir, pressing them down regularly, until you notice that the chiles have darkened a little in spots and they fill the kitchen with their spicy aroma. The whole toasting process will take 2 to 3 minutes. Scoop the chiles into a bowl, pour very hot tap water on them and lay a plate on them to keep them submerged.

2. On a broiler pan or heavy baking sheet, spread out the whole tomatillos and tomatoes and set about 4 inches under the broiler. Roast for 5 to 6 minutes until *softened* and blackened with splotches on one side (the tomatillos will have begun to turn olive green with dark spots). Use a pair of tongs to turn them over and roast for another 5 to 6 minutes until completely softened and equally darkened on the other side. Remove to cool.

3. Turn the oven down to 425 degrees. Break the onion into rings. On a similar pan or baking sheet, spread out the garlic and onion. Set in the oven and roast, stirring well every couple of minutes, until the garlic is soft and the onion richly browned—there may be a couple of charred ends here and there, but don't let it all burn or your salsa will be bitter. Total roasting time will be about 15 minutes.

OTHER DRIED CHILE POSSIBILITIES:

Guajillo, hot New Mexico, pequín, árbol, onza, costeño, pulla, pasilla.

**DISHES YOU CAN
MAKE WITH THIS
SALSA:**

Tiny Tostadas of Smoky
Chicken *Tinga* (page
43), Shrimp *Salpicón*
Salad (page 54), Chipo-
tle Mashed Potatoes
(page 63), Savory
Brunch Bread Pudding
(page 70), Spicy Veg-
etable "Stew" (page
73), Layered Tortilla
"Lasagna" with greens
and cheese (page 80),
Chile-Glazed Roast
Chicken (page 84), Pep-
pery Pan-Seared Steaks
with smoky *crema* and
blue cheese (page 94),
Smoky Glazed Ham for a
Crowd (page 102)

4. Scrape the onion and garlic into a food processor, cover and pulse until they are finely chopped but not pasty smooth. Scoop into a large bowl. Drain the rehydrated chiles (they should have soaked about 20 minutes by now—the right amount of time to soften them without soaking away too much of their flavor). For a less rustic salsa or if you're canning the salsa, peel the skins off the cooled tomatoes and cut out the "cores" where the stems were attached—always working over the baking sheet to capture all the juices. Without washing the processor, scoop in the chiles, then add the tomatillos (no need to peel off the darkened skin or cut out their cores) and tomatoes with all their accumulated juices. Pulse a few times, then let the machine run until everything is quite finely pureed (this takes a minute or so). Scrape into the bowl with the onion and garlic, then stir in the fresh thyme and enough water to give it an easily spoon-able consistency.

5. Taste, then season with salt and the sugar. Remember, like all condiments, this salsa should be highly seasoned—a little salty and with enough sugar to balance the bite of the chiles and tang of the tomatillos. **If you're planning to use your salsa right away,** simply pour it into a bowl and it's ready, or refrigerate it covered and use within 5 days. **If you're canning or freezing the salsa,** please see page 21.

STARTERS

TANGY GREEN GUACAMOLE • SALSA-BAKED GOAT CHEESE •
OPEN-FACE QUESADILLAS WITH MUSHROOMS, OLIVES,
SALSA AND GREENS • TINY TOSTADAS OF SMOKY CHICKEN
TINGA WITH AVOCADO AND AGED CHEESE • SWEET-AND-
SPICY CHILIED PORK EMPANADAS • CRISPY *MASA* BOAT
SNACKS WITH BLACK BEANS, SALSA, AVOCADO AND MEXI-
CAN CHEESE • SHRIMP IN RED ESCABECHE • MICROWAVED
"BAKED" CHIPS

Tangy Green Guacamole

Makes 3 generous cups, enough for 8 to 12 guests as a snack with chips or vegetable slices

The avocados that you use for this lusciously thick, satisfying version of the old standard should be soft enough to give under firm pressure but not be so ripe that they are easily dented or have a loose pit shaking around in them. The roasty flavors of the tomatillos, garlic and onions are the perfect way to underscore the naturally nutty flavors of avocados—especially Hass avocados, the pebbly, dark-skinned ones. Though this guacamole improves if made an hour or so ahead, it stays looking fresh and green for slightly longer than traditional guacamole (the acidity of the tomatillos helps here). But don't make it more than 3 to 4 hours in advance.

3 large ripe avocados, preferably the pebbly skinned Hass variety
1 cup Roasted Tomatillo Salsa (page 28)

¼ cup chopped fresh cilantro, plus a few leaves for garnish
Salt, about ½ teaspoon

1. Remove the little nub of stem that is usually lodged at the top of each avocado. Cut each avocado in half by slicing straight down through that spot where the stem was attached until you reach the pit, then rotate the knife all the way around the pit. Twist the two halves apart, then scoop out the pits. With a spoon, scoop out the soft flesh from the skins, collecting it in a large bowl as you go. Coarsely mash with the spoon (or use an old-fashioned potato masher or large fork).

2. Gently stir the salsa into the avocado mixture along with the chopped cilantro. Taste and season with salt. Cover with plastic wrap directly on the surface and refrigerate until you're ready to serve. (Not only will the guacamole improve if made half an hour or so before serving, but it will also maintain its fresh look longer if served cold.) Scoop the guacamole into a decorative bowl, garnish with cilantro sprigs and you're ready to set it out for your guests to enjoy.

Salsa-Baked Goat Cheese

Serves 4 to 6 as a nibble with tortilla chips, pita triangles, crackers or crispy toasts

I'd say this is one of the most perfect American appetizers for a group: warm and creamy, full of flavor, easy and spreadable. Toasted pita triangles and crisp toasts are my favorite choices to offer guests to slather this rich mixture on. No matter what you select, you'll probably find this recipe as versatile as I do.

¼ cup pine nuts or coarsely chopped walnuts or pecans

1 4-ounce log goat cheese (there are flavored goat cheeses available, some of which can be good with the salsa, but think about the flavor combination before making your purchase)

1 3-ounce package cream cheese, softened

1 cup Roasted Jalapeño-Tomato Salsa (page 23; if you like really spicy food, use the habanero variation of that salsa)

A tablespoon or so chopped fresh cilantro, for garnish

1. Heat the oven to 350 degrees. Spread out the nuts on a baking sheet and toast them in the oven until lightly browned and very fragrant, 7 or 8 minutes (the pine nuts will brown quicker than either of the others). Remove and slide them off into a medium-size bowl.

2. Add the cheeses to the bowl and combine thoroughly with the nuts. Scoop it in the center of a baking dish (I like to use a decorative 9-inch pie pan) and form it into a 5-inch-diameter disk. Spoon the salsa over and around the cheese. Place the dish in the oven and bake until heated through, 10 to 15 minutes. Sprinkle on the cilantro and set it out for your guests to enjoy as a dip or a spread.

Open-Face Quesadillas with mushrooms, olives, salsa and greens

Serves 4 as an appetizer

Two of my favorite eating experiences: standing at a street stall in Oaxaca eating a tlayuda *of crispy thin corn tortilla topped with black beans, guacamole and salsa, and sitting on the curb in front of a bakery in Rome eating a crackling thin slice of pizza with olives and mushrooms. The recipe for these open-face "quesadillas" weaves the two experiences into one, and I've added a little salad to fold up in the center, Italian* piadina-style. *Have all the ingredients ready, so that when your guests arrive you can layer and bake these stunning appetizers. Remember, these simple snacks will taste only as good as the ingredients you choose.*

4 flour tortillas
½ cup thinly sliced mushroom caps (I'd choose shiitakes for this, or during wild mushroom season, any wild mushroom I could get my hands on)
½ to ¾ cup shredded Mexican Chihuahua cheese, brick, Monterey Jack—even Cheddar or mozzarella cheese
⅓ cup roughly crumbled goat cheese
¼ cup sliced pitted olives (Kalamata or any oil-cured variety is wonderful here)

About ½ cup any salsa, plus a little more for serving if you wish
2 cups frisée leaves (broken away from the base of the head) or mixed baby greens (what's called mesclun), rinsed and dried
About 1 tablespoon fresh lime juice or vinegar (you can use any one you'd choose for a good salad dressing)
A little salt
¼ cup chopped fresh cilantro

1. Heat the oven to 500 degrees. Lightly oil a baking sheet and on it spread out the tortillas in a single layer. Distribute a portion of the mushrooms over each one, then the cheeses and olives. Drizzle 2 tablespoons of salsa over each "quesadilla," then set the baking sheet in the oven. In 5 or 6 minutes, the tortilla should be crispy underneath and the cheese melted. Remove from the oven.

2. While the quesadillas are baking, in a medium-size bowl, toss the frisée (or other greens) with the lime or vinegar, salt and cilantro. Transfer each quesadilla to a warm plate, then top with a portion of lettuce right in the center. Serve without delay.

Tiny Tostadas of Smoky Chicken *Tinga* with avocado and aged cheese

Makes 24 small tostadas, enough for 6 to 8 guests

It's rare to pass a restaurant, snack shop or street stall in the Central Mexican town of Puebla without detecting the alluring aroma of shredded pork with smoky chipotle chile, tomato and sweet onion. Tinga they call it there, and the locals spoon it into soft tacos or crusty rolls. I like to serve tinga piled onto crispy tortillas (tostadas, tostaditas or toto-pos) and topped with the typical Pueblan avocado and cheese. Though tingas are often made with chicken and pork, occasionally I go further afield to use shredded smoked fish or quail. These tostadas are the perfect accompaniment to a well-made margarita.

¾ cup Chipotle-Cascabel Salsa (page 36)

½ 15-ounce can whole tomatoes with half the can's juice

1 tablespoon vinegar, preferably cider vinegar

1 small white onion, thinly sliced

1 tablespoon vegetable or olive oil

2 cups (loosely packed) coarsely shredded cooked chicken (I'd either poach, grill or broil a large whole chicken breast or buy a small rotisserie chicken to shred)

Salt, about ½ teaspoon

24 good-size corn tortilla chips, preferably homemade thick ones

1 small ripe avocado, peeled, pitted and cut into ¼-inch dice

3 to 4 tablespoons finely grated Mexican *queso añejo*, Parmesan or Romano

Chopped fresh cilantro, for garnish

1. Combine the salsa, tomatoes with their juice and the vinegar in a blender or food processor and puree. In a large skillet, cook the onion in the oil over medium heat until crisp-tender and just beginning to brown, about 5 minutes. Press the salsa mixture through a medium-mesh strainer into the skillet. Simmer, stirring regularly, until quite thick, about 5 minutes. Stir in the chicken, cool, then taste and season with salt.

2. Arrange the chips on one or more serving platters. Top each with a heaping tablespoon of the chicken *tinga*, a few pieces of avocado, a sprinkling of cheese and a little cilantro, and they're ready to pass around.

Sweet-and-Spicy Chilied Pork Empanadas

Makes thirty to thirty-two 3-inch turnovers

When you're looking for a special appetizer (or a casual main dish), take the time to make these compellingly delicious typical Mexican turnovers. The filling of sweet-and-tangy ground pork, red chile, green olives and raisins couldn't be easier, more traditional or more delicious. Once you've tasted the filling, you'll think of many places it will fit in—sandwiches, tacos, dumplings and the like. When time won't turn you loose, replace this exceptionally tender homemade pastry with prepared, refrigerated pie dough (you'll need two 15-ounce packages). I like to set out these empanadas with a bowl of salsa or guacamole to daub on.

FOR THE DOUGH:

2¼ cups unbleached all-purpose flour

1 teaspoon baking powder

1 teaspoon salt

10 tablespoons (5 ounces) cold unsalted butter, cut into bits

5 tablespoons rich-tasting pork lard or vegetable shortening, chilled and cut into bits

1 large egg

2 to 3 tablespoons milk

. . .

1 pound ground pork (I prefer to buy 1 pound of pork shoulder and coarsely grind it in three batches in the food processor)

1 medium-size white onion, diced

1 cup Mellow Red Chile Salsa (page 30)

½ cup chopped pitted green olives (I like the straightforward flavor of Manzanillos)

½ cup raisins

2 tablespoons dark brown sugar or chopped *piloncillo* (Mexican unrefined sugar cone)

Salt, about ¾ teaspoon

1 large egg

2 tablespoons milk

1. Measure the flour, baking powder and 1 teaspoon salt into a food processor fitted with a metal blade. Process for 15 seconds to mix. Distribute the cold butter and lard or shortening over the flour mixture, connect the top and pulse until the mixture resembles coarse meal. Transfer to a large mixing bowl. In a small bowl, mix the egg with 2 *tablespoons* of the milk. Drizzle the egg mixture over the flour mixture and toss lightly with a fork just until the flour mixture is evenly moistened and can be gathered into a ball. If necessary, drizzle on the remaining *1 tablespoon* milk to moisten any dry bits. Divide the dough in half and shape each into a disk. Wrap in plastic and refrigerate at least 30 minutes, preferably 1 hour.

2. In a large skillet set over medium heat, combine the pork and onion. Cook, stirring regularly and scraping up any sticking bits, until nicely browned, about 10 minutes. Add the salsa, olives, raisins and brown sugar and continue to cook until the mixture is very thick. Taste and season with salt. Cool completely.

3. Heat the oven to 400 degrees. Grease 2 baking sheets or line them with parchment paper. On a lightly floured work surface, roll out half of the dough into a rectangle 16 x 12 inches (it should be about 1/16 inch thick). Cut out fifteen 3-inch circles. With a pastry brush dipped into cold water, *very lightly* paint the edges of each circle. Scoop about 1 tablespoon of the filling onto each circle, fold over and press the edges together with the tines of a fork. Transfer to the baking sheets, arranging them about one inch apart. (If you have time, slide these into the freezer for 30 minutes to ensure that the dough won't shrink as it bakes.) Repeat with the remaining dough and filling. Beat the egg and 2 tablespoons milk together. Lightly paint the empanadas with an even coating of the egg mixture, being careful not to let it run down on the baking sheets (it will make them stick). Bake until richly golden, 15 to 18 minutes. Serve warm or at room temperature.

Crispy *Masa Boat* Snacks with black beans, salsa, avocado and Mexican cheese

· · · · ·

Makes 20, serving 10 as
a pass-around appetizer
or little snack

These are the classic little sopes from Central and West-Central Mexico but with a twist—they're baked rather than fried. And if you take care when forming the little boats, they'll be one of the prettiest, tastiest pass-around appetizers you can make. Earthy black beans against golden corny masa, *jazzed up with a splash of robust salsa, a dot of creamy avocado and the spring-fresh burst of cilantro. These are toppings I like, but feel free to let your mind roam to other full-flavored options like Chorizo and Black Bean Chili (page 96), the pork filling for Empanadas (page 44), even Tangy Green Guacamole (page 40). It's best to have all the toppings prepared when the sopes go into the oven. Bake them just before serving.*

½ pound (1 cup) freshly ground corn *masa* for tortillas (you'll have to get this at a tortilla factory or well-stocked Mexican grocery)
OR 1 cup *masa harina* mixed with ½ cup plus 2 tablespoons hot water
2½ tablespoons rich-tasting pork lard or vegetable oil
1 teaspoon baking powder
¼ teaspoon salt, plus a little more for the beans if they need it
¾ cup finely grated Mexican *queso añejo*, Parmesan or Romano
2 large egg yolks

1½ cups cooked black beans with their liquid
½ medium-size white onion, finely chopped and rinsed briefly under cold water
½ cup Roasted Poblano-Tomato Salsa (page 26)
1 large ripe avocado, peeled, pitted and diced
¼ cup chopped fresh cilantro

1. Heat the oven to 350 degrees. Lightly grease a baking sheet. In a large bowl, mix together the *masa* or reconstituted *masa harina* with the lard or oil, baking powder, salt, ½ *cup* of the cheese and the egg yolks. The mixture should be the consistency of a medium-soft cookie dough. Divide into 20 balls, flatten each one into a 2-inch disk, then pinch up a ¼-inch-high border all around. Arrange the *sopes* on the baking sheet, then bake until lightly browned and crispy, 17 to 20 minutes.

2. While the *sopes* are baking, warm the black beans in a small saucepan with just enough of their liquid to cover the bottom of the pan—the beans should not be covered by the liquid. Use a fork or potato masher to coarsely mash the beans into a thickish mass that easily holds its shape in a spoon. Taste and season with salt.

3. Spoon a portion of the black beans into each of the *sopes,* then top with a little chopped onion, a small spoonful of salsa and a couple pieces of avocado. Sprinkle everything with the remaining ¼ *cup* cheese and the cilantro, and you're ready to set your warm, crispy nibbles on a platter to pass among your guests.

Shrimp in Red Escabeche

Serves 4 to 6 as an appetizer

If you like the lusty earthiness of barbecued shrimp, this is the dish for you. Zesty, sweet and spicy shrimp with plenty of red chile, red onion slivers and cilantro leaves to remind you that you're on Mexican terrain. Though this dish is often served warm in its homeland in Northeastern Mexico, I like it cool—as I've described here—to pass around as a kind of lick-your-fingers nibble before a special dinner. If the weather's hot, serve Shrimp in Red Escabeche with a leafy salad as the main attraction. Escabeche, by the way, describes many traditional preparations in which vinegar is used to preserve the main ingredients.

1½ cups Roasty Red Guajillo Salsa (page 33)
2 tablespoons olive oil
1½ tablespoons cider vinegar
1 tablespoon honey or more to taste
Salt, about ½ teaspoon

1 pound medium-large (about 24) shrimp, peeled (I'd leave on the last segment and the tail) and deveined
1 small red onion, thinly sliced
½ cup fresh cilantro leaves

1. Puree the salsa in a blender and press through a medium-mesh strainer into a bowl. Heat the olive oil in a large skillet (I prefer a 12-inch nonstick skillet) over medium. Add the salsa and briskly simmer, stirring frequently, until cooked down to the consistency of tomato paste (it should reduce enough for the oil to rise, leaving a sheen on the surface), 3 or 4 minutes. Remove from the heat and stir in the vinegar. Taste and season with honey and salt—it should taste slightly salty and have a hint of sweetness.

2. Stir the shrimp into the cooked salsa (there should be just enough to coat everything lightly) and return the skillet to medium heat. Cook, stirring constantly, until the shrimp are just barely cooked through (cut open a shrimp to see that it has turned from translucent to opaque white), about 3 minutes. Scoop onto a platter and let cool to room temperature. In a small strainer, rinse the sliced onion under cold water and shake until nearly dry. Sprinkle over the shrimp along with the cilantro leaves, and the dish is ready to serve.

Microwaved "Baked" Chips

Makes 72 chips, enough
for 4 to 8 snackers

There's really no substitute for freshly fried chips. I say that from experience, having sampled tortilla chips fresh from our restaurant fryer for years and years. Though I've written recipes in other books for fried chips, these days lots of us are interested in chips that have less contact with oil. So here's a nice, light, toothsome chip (perhaps not as tender as fried chips) that'll taste fresh and corny.

12 corn tortillas (see Note)
Vegetable oil for brushing or misting

Salt, preferably kosher or sea salt

1. Lay the tortillas out on your cutting board, lightly brush or mist both sides with oil, then cut each tortilla into 6 wedges. Lay the wedges out in a single layer on the bottom of your microwave oven (mine has a removable tray that completely covers the bottom, so arranging the tortillas is easy to do on the countertop).

2. Microwave on high for 1½ minutes. Turn the tortilla wedges over and microwave for another 1½ minutes. Continue turning and microwaving at 1½-minute intervals, moving the wedges around if some seem to be browning more than others, until they are crisp (remember, as they cool, they'll crisp even more). Total microwaving time in my not-very-new 700-watt microwave is about 7½ minutes (five 1½-minute intervals). Immediately toss the chips with salt and they're ready to serve.

Note: Your corn tortilla choice is very important. Made with the very coarse-textured, commercialized brands you find in most refrigerated food cases, these chips will taste like cardboard and have a heavy, uninteresting texture. Thick, fresh corn tortillas from a local factory—the kind sold at Mexican groceries in Mexican communities—are wonderful for eating hot and steamy with a meal. For chips, they take longer to "bake," they "bake" more unevenly, and they separate into layers which to my mind makes them seem shatteringly brittle. My favorite tortilla for these "baked" chips is a *thin*, fresh corn tortilla from one of our local factories (in Chicago, I choose the thinner La Mexicana brand tortillas that are sold in the plastic wrappers, not their thicker tortillas in the paper wrappers).

SOUPS, SALADS AND SIDE DISHES

GREAT TORTILLA SOUP • EMERALD CORN CHOWDER WITH ROASTED TOMATILLOS AND POBLANO • SHRIMP *SALPICÓN* SALAD WITH POTATOES, AVOCADOS AND CHIPOTLE • RED CHILE-JÍCAMA SALAD WITH ORANGE AND RED ONION • POBLANO-ROASTED VEGETABLE SALAD WITH PEPPERY WATERCRESS • TANGY LENTIL SALAD WITH SPINACH, CILANTRO AND CHAYOTE • GUAJILLO GRILLED VEGETABLES • CLASSIC RED TOMATO RICE • CHIPOTLE MASHED POTATOES • SCALLOPED POTATOES WITH ROASTED TOMATILLOS, SERRANOS AND CILANTRO

Great Tortilla Soup

Serves 6 generously

In our restaurant Topolobampo, we begin by arranging the classic adornments for this soup in wide-rimmed soup bowls. The cheese goes in first, followed by the tortilla strips and avocado, then a dollop of cream and a little crushed dried chile are added for good measure. At the table, we ladle in the dark, aromatic broth, letting it flood around the tasty morsels. If you want drama and elegance, follow our lead. For ease, add the garnishes to the soup in the kitchen. Or for fun, pile all the adornments onto a big platter and let guests help themselves.

1 tablespoon olive oil
3 cups Mellow Red Chile Salsa (page 30)
4 cups rich-tasting chicken broth
Vegetable oil to a depth of ½ inch,
    for frying
6 to 8 corn tortillas, cut into ¼-inch strips
Salt, about ½ teaspoon if you're using un-
    salted broth

1 cup (about 4 ounces) shredded
    Mexican Chihuahua cheese,
    Monterey Jack or Cheddar
1 large ripe avocado, peeled, pitted
    and diced
1 to 2 limes, cut into wedges

1. In a large saucepan or soup pot, heat the olive oil over medium-high until it is very hot. Add the salsa and stir continuously until it is cooked down to a thick paste, about 10 minutes. Add the chicken broth, partially cover and simmer over medium-low heat for 45 minutes.

2. While the soup is gently bubbling along, heat the vegetable oil in a small skillet over medium to medium-high. When a strip of tortilla sizzles riotously in the oil, add about one-third of the strips, fry until crispy (they'll almost stop sizzling when they're ready), scoop out with tongs or a slotted spoon and drain on paper towels. In two batches, fry and drain the remaining tortilla strips in the same fashion.

3. Taste the soup and season it with salt if necessary. Ladle into warm bowls and top each with a portion of shredded cheese (scatter it around so it dissolves evenly), a few cubes of avocado and a portion of the tortilla strips. Carry the bowls to the table along with the lime wedges for each guest to squeeze into the soup to their liking.

Emerald Corn Chowder with roasted tomatillos and poblano

• • • • •

Makes about 6 cups, serving 4 to 6

The roasty vegetable flavors in this zesty soup are sweetened with masa, *the dough that's used for making corn tortillas. Whether you use the easily accessible dehydrated* masa harina *or the fresh dough available from tortilla factories, you'll love the complex flavor and texture it brings to this soup. Dress up your soup with grilled shrimp or scallops to start a very special meal—even drizzle on a little crème fraîche right before serving—or consider using the soup as a sauce for grilled fresh fish or vegetables. This preparation is remarkably versatile. It's based on a classic soup from Central and Eastern Mexico that's called* chileatole.

1 small white onion, sliced ¼ inch thick
1 large fresh poblano chile, stemmed, seeded and roughly chopped
1 tablespoon vegetable or olive oil
2 cups corn kernels, preferably freshly cut off the cobs (you'll need about 3 ears)
2 cups Roasted Tomatillo Salsa (page 28)

2½ cups rich-tasting chicken broth
2 tablespoons fresh corn *masa* for tortillas (you'll have to get this at a tortilla factory or well-stocked Mexican grocery)
OR 2 tablespoons *masa harina*
Salt, about ½ teaspoon
½ cup chopped fresh cilantro

1. In a large saucepan or soup pot, cook the onion and poblano in the oil over medium heat until both are tender, 5 to 6 minutes. Scrape into a blender or food processor and add *half* of the corn and all of the salsa. Process to a smooth puree and press through a medium-mesh strainer back into the pan or pot.

2. Stir in the broth, partially cover and simmer over low heat, stirring often, for 30 minutes. In a small bowl, mix the *masa* or *masa harina* with ¼ cup water, making sure there are no lumps. Strain the mixture (you can use the same strainer) directly into the simmering pot, stirring until the soup thickens to the consistency of cream soup. Taste and season with salt. Add the remaining *1 cup* corn kernels, let return to a simmer, then ladle into warm bowls. Sprinkle with the chopped cilantro before carrying the soup to the table.

Shrimp Salpicón Salad with potatoes, avocados and chipotle

Serves 6

Salpicón *refers to a variety of meat-and-potato salads made in Central Mexico, the best known being flavored with little strips of smoky chipotle chiles. I've stretched the definition of these classic salads to include shrimp here, as well as an exciting dressing that weaves in the chipotle flavor. Carry this salpicón on a picnic or set it out on a buffet; it's a terrific warm-weather choice. The word salpicón literally means a bright little splash of seasoning.*

5 medium-size (about 1¼ pounds) boiling potatoes (like the red-skinned ones), peeled and cut into ½-inch cubes

4 medium carrots, peeled and cut into ½-inch cubes

1½ cups Chipotle-Cascabel Salsa (page 36)

¼ cup fruity olive oil

1 tablespoon cider vinegar, plus a little more if you think the salad needs it

¼ teaspoon salt

¼ teaspoon freshly ground black pepper

1½ pounds medium-large (about 23) shrimp, peeled and deveined

1 large ripe tomato, cored and cut into ½-inch pieces

Lettuce leaves for serving (butter lettuce is beautiful here)

2 ripe avocados, peeled, pitted and cut into ½-inch dice

3 canned chipotle chiles *en adobo*, seeded and thinly sliced

Several tablespoons chopped fresh cilantro, for garnish

1. In a medium-size saucepan, bring several inches of water to a boil, heavily salt it, and add the potatoes and carrots. Cook at a gentle boil (medium heat is right here) until the vegetables are just tender (they should be firm but not crunchy), about 7 minutes. Drain well and cool.

2. Measure the salsa into a large skillet (at least 12 inches or use 2 medium-size skillets). Stir in the oil, vinegar, salt and pepper. Set over medium heat and stir regularly as the salsa mixture gently boils and reduces slightly, 5 to 6 minutes. Increase the heat to medium-high and add the shrimp. Stir continuously, turning the shrimp to coat them with the salsa mixture, until just barely cooked through (cut open a shrimp to see that it has turned from translucent to opaque white), 3 to 4 minutes. With a pair of tongs or a slotted spoon, remove the shrimp to a large plate, leaving behind as much salsa mixture as possible. Spread out the shrimp in a single layer to stop their cooking. Let the salsa cool in the skillet, then fold in the potatoes, carrots and tomato. If there is time, let the mixture stand for 30 minutes or so to allow the vegetables to absorb the flavors.

3. Just before serving, fold the shrimp into the salsa mixture. Line either a serving platter or individual plates with lettuce leaves. Gently scoop on the shrimp salad, decorate with pieces of avocado and strips of chipotle chiles, then sprinkle with cilantro. You're ready to set the salad before your guests.

Red Chile-Jícama Salad with orange and red onion

Serves about 6

When you turn practically any corner in practically any Mexican town, a street vendor will be there with slabs of juicy, crunchy jícama drizzled with lime and dusted with hot powdered chile. That classic tangy, spicy, juicy-fresh crunch is what we've captured in this salad—brought in off the streets and dressed up for company. When I'm grilling, jícama always comes to mind as a starter; with the grill already going, charcoal-searing slices of fresh pineapple makes a fantastic addition to this salad. Don't hesitate to prepare the salad several hours in advance (minus lettuce and cilantro, of course) and keep it refrigerated until you're ready to serve.

3 oranges
½ cup Mellow Red Chile Salsa (page 30)
¼ cup fresh lime juice
Salt, about 1 teaspoon
1 small (1-pound) jícama, peeled and cut into ¾-inch cubes
1 medium-size red onion, thinly sliced

½ small fresh pineapple, peeled, cored, and cut into 1-inch pieces (optional)
1 small head romaine, tough outer leaves removed, inner leaves sliced crosswise ½ inch wide
½ cup chopped fresh cilantro

1. With a zester or vegetable peeler, remove the zest (colored peel only) from half of an orange. Finely mince the zest and transfer it to a large stainless steel or glass bowl. Add the salsa (I usually take the time to first puree it and press it through a medium-mesh strainer to remove all the skins) and lime juice to the orange zest. Taste and season with salt (it should be a little salty). Add the jícama and onion, toss to mix well, then let stand for about 30 minutes.

2. Cut the stem and blossom ends from all the oranges, then standing each orange on a cutting board and working close to the flesh, cut away the rind and all the white pith. Cut the oranges into ¼-inch-thick slices. Cut the slices into quarters.

3. Stir the orange pieces and optional pineapple into the jícama mixture. Divide the lettuce between individual serving plates, forming it into a rough nest shape. Pile the marinated jícama mixture in the middle. Sprinkle everything with cilantro.

Poblano-Roasted Vegetable Salad with peppery watercress

Serves 6

Why do we all love roasted vegetables so much? Perhaps it's their sweetness, since the browned edges that roasting brings taste darkly sugary on the tongue. Roasted is the way I learned to love beets, and for this salad I encourage you to choose the candy-stripe or golden beets available at most farmers' markets. Their lighter colors are particularly beautiful—though red beets, while they color whatever they touch, are delicious, too. Think of this rich saucy dressing for other salads—especially potato salad with smoked mussels or clams—or shrimp cocktail.

2 cups Roasted Poblano-Tomato Salsa (page 26)
¼ cup fruity olive oil
5 tablespoons fresh lime juice
Salt, about ¾ teaspoon, plus a little extra for the watercress
3 medium (10 ounces total) beets, scrubbed, roots trimmed off, each cut into 8 wedges

3 medium (12 ounces total) Yukon gold potatoes, scrubbed, each cut into 6 wedges
2 heads (1 pound total) fresh fennel, tops cut off, each cut into 8 wedges
3 bunches watercress, large stems cut off
Crumbled *queso fresco* or salted farmer's cheese, for garnish

1. Heat the oven to 375 degrees. Combine *half* of the salsa, the olive oil and 3 *tablespoons* of the lime juice. Taste this marinade and season with salt (it should be salty to season the vegetables as they roast). In another bowl, combine the beets and potatoes with two-thirds of the marinade.

2. In a large roasting pan, toss the fennel with the remaining marinade, spread in a single layer, cover with foil and bake for 25 minutes, until nearly tender when pierced with a fork. Uncover, add the marinated beets and potatoes in a single layer, then re-cover and return to the oven for 15 minutes. Uncover and continue to roast, turning, stirring and basting all the vegetables every few minutes, until they are tender and browned, about 20 minutes. Cool.

3. Toss the watercress with the remaining 2 *tablespoons* lime juice mixed with a little salt and divide between 6 salad plates. Arrange the vegetables beside the watercress and spoon a portion of the remaining 1 cup salsa over them. Crumble the cheese on top and serve.

Tangy Lentil Salad with spinach, cilantro and chayote

Serves 8 as a salad or accompaniment

When the Spaniards brought lentils, favas and garbanzos to a New World that already relied heavily on kidney, pinto and black beans for sustenance, they were adopted enthusiastically. If you cook the firm-textured dark green Le Puy (or the fabulous-tasting black beluga) lentils and mix them with this delicious salsa dressing made tangy with tomatillos and lime, you'll have a salad that's perfect for a first course, light main course or summer picnic. We've added the wonderfully crunchy texture and sweet taste of chayote here, set the mixture in a nest of spinach and dusted it all with the very Mexican queso añejo. I think it's just about the most perfect non-lettuce salad you can make.

2 cups (about 12 ounces) lentils, preferably Le Puy green lentils (or perhaps those very special small black lentils they call "beluga" after the caviar)

1¼ cups Roasted Tomatillo Salsa (page 28)

¼ cup olive oil, preferably a good-tasting fruity one

2 tablespoons fresh lime juice

½ cup chopped fresh cilantro

½ teaspoon salt, plus a little more for the vegetables

1 medium-size white onion, sliced

2 small (about 12 ounces total) chayotes, cut into ¼-inch slices (peel, seed and all), then into ¼-inch strips

2 medium-size ripe tomatoes, diced

8 cups (about 10 ounces) stemmed "salad" spinach (small smooth leaves), well rinsed

½ cup finely grated Mexican *queso añejo*, Parmesan or Romano

I. Bring a good-size pot of water to a boil over high heat, salt it generously and sprinkle in the lentils. When the water returns to the boil, reduce the heat to medium and let cook at a lively simmer until the lentils are tender to the core but not falling apart, 15 to 20 minutes for green lentils, less for most other varieties. Drain well and pour into a bowl.

2. In a food processor or blender, combine the salsa, 2 *tablespoons* of the oil, the lime juice, cilantro and salt. Process until the dressing is very smooth. Stir half of the dressing into the warm lentils and set aside.

3. Heat the remaining 2 *tablespoons* oil in a large skillet over medium-high. Add the onion and chayote strips and stir-fry until nicely browned but still a little crunchy, about 10 minutes. Sprinkle with a little salt, scoop into a wide bowl and stir in half of the remaining dressing. Cool to room temperature, then mix with the lentils and *half* of the tomatoes. Taste and season with salt if necessary.

4. If the spinach is wet, you'll need to dry it on towels (paper or otherwise) or by using a salad spinner. In a large bowl, toss the spinach with the remaining dressing and divide it between serving plates, making a little nest of it. (Alternatively, you can arrange the spinach on a large platter.) Nestle a portion of the lentil salad into each bed of spinach (or all of it into the larger bed), sprinkle with the grated cheese and a little of the remaining chopped tomato, and you're ready to serve.

Guajillo Grilled Vegetables

Serves 8 as an accompaniment

When the farmers' markets are heaped with the best variety, outdoor cooking is at its most inviting. So buy what's there, lay it on the grill and bring it alive with this red-chile baste, a shower of fresh herbs and a squirt of lime. If you have an oil mister, this recipe is a good place to use it: the mister coats your vegetables with a more even, lighter coating of oil than a basting brush.

½ cup Roasty Red Guajillo Salsa (page 33)

About 6 tablespoons olive oil, preferably a good-tasting fruity one

1½ tablespoons vinegar, such as a rich red wine or balsamic vinegar

½ teaspoon salt, plus a little more for each vegetable

1 pint small ripe cherry tomatoes, stemmed

2 small (14 ounces total) sweet potatoes, peeled and each cut into 4 long slices

4 medium (1¼ pounds total) zucchini or yellow summer squash, stem ends removed and each cut into 4 long slices

2 small (about 12 ounces total) chayote, peeled and each cut into 4 long slices

1 medium (1-pound) eggplant, stem end removed, cut into 4 long slices, then each slice cut crosswise in half

2 small bunches green onions, roots and wilted greens removed

A tablespoon or two of chopped fresh herbs, such as thyme, oregano, basil (you'll likely want more than a couple of tablespoons of basil) or flat-leaf parsley

2 limes, cut into wedges

1. Light a charcoal fire and let it burn until the coals are medium-hot and covered with gray ash, about 20 minutes; or preheat a gas grill on high for 10 minutes, then reduce the heat to medium.

2. Combine the salsa, 2 *tablespoons* of the oil, the vinegar and ½ *teaspoon* salt in a blender. Process to as smooth a mixture as possible. Pour the remaining oil into a small dish (or use a mister) and set it beside the grill, along with the salsa mixture, 2 basting brushes and some salt. Toss the cherry tomatoes with a little of the oil in a small bowl.

3. When the grill is ready, brush or mist the cooking grates lightly with oil, then one by one brush or mist the vegetable slices and green onions with oil and lay them on the grill. (Do this in batches if necessary so the grill is not crowded.) Sprinkle with salt, cover the grill and cook for

5 minutes. Uncover, flip the slices over and baste heavily with the salsa mixture. Cover and cook for 3 or 4 minutes longer, basting with salsa again if you wish. Uncover and begin transferring (in a decorative manner) the slices to the platter as they are done: the zucchini, chayote and green onions should be just about tender but still have good texture, the eggplant will be cooked to the center in a couple of minutes, while the sweet potatoes will be the last to cook through.

4. When space permits, roll the tomatoes onto the grill to warm them through and give them a little flavor (if they spend too long there, their skins will burst), then use a pair of tongs to remove them to the platter with the other vegetables. Strew with chopped herbs, decorate with the lime wedges and carry to the table. Encourage your guests to squeeze lime on the vegetables before they feast.

Classic Red Tomato Rice

Makes about 6 cups,
serving 6 to 8

There's scarcely a soul, I'm sure, that hasn't eaten the mealy, near-tasteless red rice at a run-of-the-mill Mexican-American restaurant. The red rice that results from this recipe is a world away from that, especially if you use medium-grain rice, which has a wonderfully toothsome texture. Roasted Jalapeño-Tomato Salsa adds real pizzazz, and the technique of browning the raw rice (typical of pilaf-style rice making) lends a complex toastiness and ensures separate grains. In fact, this rice is so good, you can serve it with a piece of grilled or broiled fish or a bowl of savory, long-simmered beans and you'll feel the meal is complete. Look for medium-grain rice in Mexican groceries or substitute Italian arborio *rice or Valencian* paella *rice, though the latter two options are more expensive.*

2 tablespoons vegetable or olive oil
2 cups rice, preferably medium grain
2 cups Roasted Jalapeño-Tomato Salsa
  (page 23)

1½ cups hot chicken broth or water
1 teaspoon salt
½ cup chopped fresh cilantro

1. Heat the oven to 350 degrees. In a 3-quart, ovenproof saucepan, heat the oil over medium. Add the rice and cook, stirring regularly, until almost all the kernels have turned from translucent to milky white and have begun to brown, about 5 minutes. Add the salsa and cook, stirring, for 1 minute, then add the broth or water and salt. Bring to a boil, stir once and scrape down the rice kernels that are clinging to the side of the pan.

2. Cover tightly and bake for 25 minutes. Remove from the oven, uncover and test a few rice kernels; they should be just about tender at the core (if not, return the saucepan to the oven for a few minutes longer). Re-cover the pot and let stand off the heat on the back of the stove for 5 to 10 minutes to finish cooking. Uncover, sprinkle with the cilantro and use a fork to fluff everything together—there will be a layer of tomato that's risen to the top that you'll need to mix back in.

Chipotle Mashed Potatoes

Serves 6

Puré de papa (*puree of potatoes*) they call it in Mexico, and they spoon it on plate after plate in coffee shops and everyday restaurants all through the republic. Most North Americans have trouble believing this, fixed on the image of beans-and-rice as we are. But Mexicans love mashed potatoes, finding them as comforting as we do. Here we're offering a new version, perhaps more of a main attraction than a supporting player, as they are jazzed up with smoky chipotles, roasted tomatillos and garlic. This version is easy to make and fabulous with grilled chicken or steak; Thanksgiving dinner just may never be the same. I prefer this recipe made with the buttery-tasting, denser-textured Yukon gold potatoes rather than the lighter-flavored, fluffy russets often used for mashed potatoes. My second choice: the even creamier red-skinned boiling potatoes, but then I like that unctuous consistency.

8 medium (2 pounds total) Yukon gold or
   red-skinned potatoes, peeled if you wish
   (scrub them well if you're not peeling
   them) and cut into 1½-inch chunks
½ cup Chipotle-Cascabel Salsa (page 36)

½ cup milk or half-and-half
4 to 6 tablespoons softened butter
¼ cup chopped fresh cilantro
Salt, about 1 teaspoon

1. In a large saucepan, simmer the potatoes in heavily salted water to cover over medium heat until fork-tender, about 20 minutes. Drain the potatoes thoroughly and return them to the pan.

2. Set the pan over medium heat and add the salsa, milk or half-and-half, butter and cilantro. Mash with an old-fashioned potato masher until they are the texture you like (I prefer this robust version of mashed potatoes still rather coarse and chunky). Taste and season with salt, then scoop into a warm bowl to pass at the table.

Scalloped Potatoes with roasted tomatillos, serranos and cilantro

Serves 8 as a side dish

Scalloped potatoes are one of my favorite side dishes and have been since my early days at church suppers and Sunday dinners at grandma's. And not all their magnetism has to come from luscious cream, cheese and butter. Here we draw you in with a full-flavored sauce of roasted tomatillo salsa, milk and corn masa, and I recommend using the buttery-tasting Yukon gold potatoes. Layer the dish immediately after thinly slicing the potatoes (soaking them in water to prevent discoloring will turn out a watery dish) and be sure to bake it until the potatoes are completely tender.

1½ cups milk
3 tablespoons freshly ground corn *masa* for tortillas (you'll have to get this at a tortilla factory or well-stocked Mexican grocery)
   OR 3 tablespoons *masa harina*
1½ cups Roasted Tomatillo Salsa (page 28)
Salt, about 1 teaspoon

12 medium-large (3 pounds total) boiling potatoes (red-skinned ones work well here, as do the more all-purpose Yukon golds), sliced ⅛ inch thick
1½ cups (about 6 ounces) shredded Mexican Chihuahua cheese, brick, Monterey Jack or Cheddar

1. Heat the oven to 325 degrees. In a blender or food processor, combine the milk and *masa* or *masa harina* and process until thoroughly combined. Pour into a medium-size saucepan, set over medium-high heat and whisk constantly—to avoid getting any lumps—until the mixture comes to a boil, about 10 minutes. Whisk in the salsa, then taste and season the sauce with salt.

2. Generously butter or oil a 13 x 9-inch baking dish, then spread *half* of the potatoes evenly over the bottom. Spoon half of the tomatillo sauce over the potatoes, then sprinkle on *half* of the cheese. Repeat with another layer of potatoes, sauce and cheese.

3. Bake uncovered until the potatoes are tender when you put a fork into them and the cheese is a beautiful crusty brown, 50 to 60 minutes. Let stand for 10 minutes before serving.

Poblano-Roasted Vegetable Salad with

peppery watercress (page 57)

Racy Eggplant Omelet with
savory red chile (page 66)

Red Chile Pasta (page 71)

Today's Macaroni and Cheese—
it's not just for kids (page 72)

Layered Tortilla "Lasagna" with
greens and cheese (page 80)   13

Soft Tacos of Grilled Chicken Breast with
tangy green chile and grilled onions (page 86)

Peppery Pan-Seared Steaks with
smoky *crema* and blue cheese (page 94)

Spicy Jalapeño Beef Tips (page 97)

EGG, VEGETABLE, PASTA AND TORTILLA MAIN COURSES

RACY EGGPLANT OMELETS WITH SAVORY RED CHILE · OPEN-FACE CHORIZO-POTATO OMELET WITH TOMATILLO SALSA · BREAKFAST ENCHILADAS OF SCRAMBLED EGGS, WOODLAND MUSHROOMS AND SPICY ROASTED TOMATOES · SAVORY BRUNCH BREAD PUDDING · RED CHILE PASTA · TODAY'S MACARONI AND CHEESE—IT'S NOT JUST FOR KIDS · SPICY VEGETABLE "STEW" · TOASTY *FIDEOS* (VERMICELLI) WITH ROASTED TOMATO, BLACK BEANS AND CHARD · *CHILAQUILES* (TORTILLA CASSEROLE) WITH SPINACH, ZUCCHINI AND AGED CHEESE · SEARED RED-CHILE ENCHILADAS WITH CHICKEN AND AGED CHEESE · LAYERED TORTILLA "LASAGNA" WITH GREENS AND CHEESE

Racy Eggplant Omelets with savory red chile

Serves 4

I carry with me a compellingly vivid, tasty memory of a Szechuan eggplant dish from years ago. And with this recipe I've gotten pretty close to what I remember of that flavor by seasoning quick-fried eggplant with red chile salsa, soy and chipotles (bacon drippings are an easy way to replace the pork in my taste memory). Roll this thrillingly spicy mixture into an omelet, drizzle it with salsa, and you have a meal that spunky friends will eat up.

About 5 tablespoons bacon drippings, butter or vegetable or olive oil
1 medium-size white onion, diced
1 medium (1-pound) eggplant, stem end removed, cut into ½-inch cubes
1 cup Mellow Red Chile Salsa (page 30)
1 tablespoon soy sauce

½ to 1½ tablespoons chopped canned chipotle chiles *en adobo* (optional)
Salt, about 1 teaspoon
8 large eggs
¼ cup water or milk
Several tablespoons chopped fresh cilantro, for garnish

1. In a large (12-inch) skillet, preferably nonstick, heat 3 *tablespoons* of the bacon drippings (or their stand-in) over medium. Add the onion and cook until translucent, 3 to 4 minutes. Stir in the eggplant and cook, stirring regularly, until the eggplant is browned and soft—to the point that it is almost falling apart—about 15 minutes. Stir in ¼ *cup* of the salsa, the soy sauce and optional chipotles. Season with salt (*about ¼ teaspoon*) and remove from heat.

2. Turn the oven on to its lowest setting. In a medium-size bowl, lightly beat the eggs with the water or milk and *about ½ teaspoon* salt. Heat a smallish nonstick or well-seasoned skillet or omelet pan over medium-high. When quite hot, add ½ *tablespoon* of the remaining bacon drippings (or other choice), let heat a few seconds, then add one-quarter of the egg mixture. Stir every few seconds to create large curds, and when creamy but set enough to hold together, spoon one-quarter of the eggplant across the center. Immediately roll the omelet out onto a serving plate and keep warm in the oven. Prepare remaining omelets in the same fashion.

3. When all the omelets are made, spoon a generous 2 or 3 tablespoons of salsa in a decorative ribbon across each one, sprinkle with the chopped cilantro and whisk away to the table.

Open-Face Chorizo-Potato Omelet with tomatillo salsa

. . . . .

Makes 4 good-size servings

This open-face (or frittata-style) omelet is lazy Sunday morning food at our house, the kind of dish my daughter, Lanie, and I make after we've walked to the corner store to see what's left by the Saturday shoppers (thank goodness the store always has chorizo and tomatillos!). It's easy, substantial enough to call brunch, and any leftovers are wonderful at room temperature later in the day. Serve your zesty treat with thick slabs of crusty bread or warm corn tortillas and fresh fruit or a salad.

1½ tablespoons vegetable or olive oil
1 medium-size white onion, diced
½ cup (4 ounces) raw Mexican chorizo
  sausage, casing removed
6 small (about 12 ounces total) boiling
  potatoes (like the red-skinned ones),
  scrubbed, each cut into 8 pieces

4 large eggs
Salt, about ½ teaspoon
¾ cup Roasted Tomatillo Salsa (page 28)
2 or 3 tablespoons finely grated
  Mexican *queso añejo,* Parmesan
  or Romano

1. Heat the oven to 375 degrees. In a 10-inch, ovenproof, nonstick skillet, heat the oil over medium. Add the onion and chorizo; cook, stirring regularly and breaking up the chorizo, until the onion is soft, about 7 minutes. Mix in the potatoes, cover and continue to cook, stirring from time to time, until the onion is lightly browned and the potatoes are soft, about 10 minutes. Reduce heat to medium-low and pour off excess fat if more than 1 tablespoon.

2. In a small bowl, beat together the eggs, a scant ½ teaspoon salt and ½ *cup* of the salsa. Pour this mixture into the pan, stir everything around several times to coat the potatoes with the egg mixture, then let stand over the heat for a couple of minutes until the egg mixture is set underneath. Place in the oven and bake until just set, about 4 minutes.

3. In one quick swoop, slide the omelet onto a warm serving plate and cut into quarters. Splash with the remaining ¼ *cup* salsa, sprinkle with the cheese and serve immediately.

Breakfast Enchiladas of scrambled eggs, woodland mushrooms and spicy roasted tomatoes

• • • • •

Serves 4

Hot corn tortillas with eggs have always provided me the same elemental gustatory pleasure as a crusty grilled cheese sandwich. The logical culinary development of this pairing leads directly to enchiladas: the tortillas rolled around eggs and baked under a light blanket of tasty salsa and melted cheese. I've chosen to scramble the eggs here with woodsy mushrooms (and goat cheese in my kitchen), a wonderful regional touch I've tasted at roadside stands in the mountainous forests around Mexico City.

10 corn tortillas, preferably store-bought
2¾ cups Roasted Jalapeño-Tomato Salsa (page 23)
3 cups (about 6 ounces) sliced stemmed mushrooms (choose ones like the flavorful cultivated shiitakes or wild morels, chanterelles or hedgehogs), well rinsed
2 teaspoons finely chopped fresh thyme (optional)
1 tablespoon olive oil or butter

6 large eggs, lightly beaten
Scant ½ teaspoon salt
⅔ cup crumbled fresh goat cheese or cream cheese (optional)
1 cup (4 ounces) shredded Cheddar cheese or other easily melted cheese like Mexican Chihuahua or Monterey Jack
Chopped fresh cilantro, for garnish

1. Heat the oven to 400 degrees. Wrap the tortillas in a clean kitchen towel, lay the package in a steamer with about 1 inch of water at the bottom, set the lid in place and bring the water to a strong boil for 1 minute. Remove the pan from the heat and let stand, covered, for 15 minutes.

2. In a large skillet (preferably nonstick), combine ¾ *cup* of the salsa with the mushrooms, optional thyme and the oil or butter. Cover (you may have to borrow a cover from another pot), set over medium heat and cook for 7 or 8 minutes, until the mushrooms are stewing well in their juices. Uncover and cook, stirring frequently, until the mixture is nearly dry, 2 to 3 minutes longer. Raise the heat to medium-high, and when the mixture is sizzling away, add the beaten eggs and the salt. Stir every few seconds until the eggs are *barely* set—still very creamy. Remove immediately from the heat and stir in the optional goat cheese or cream cheese.

3. Spoon ½ *cup* of the remaining salsa over the bottom of an 11 x 7-inch baking dish. One by one, remove a hot tortilla from the towel, spoon on a portion of the filling, roll up and place seam side down in the baking dish. You'll need 8 filled tortillas; there are 2 extra in case some break up.

4. Spoon the remaining 1½ *cups* salsa over the enchiladas, making sure to completely cover the tortillas, then sprinkle with the Cheddar (or other) cheese. Bake just until the cheese is melted and the sauce hot, about 20 minutes. Let stand for 5 minutes, then sprinkle with cilantro and serve.

Savory Brunch Bread Pudding

Serves 9 to 12 as an accompaniment, about 6 as a main dish

This rich-tasting savory bread pudding is usually gone before anything else on a brunch buffet. It's creamy, spicy, a little cheesy, with a hint of smokiness. Studded with cubes of good ham is the way I like this bread pudding best, and made with ham it's great for a casual (or buffet) lunch or supper. Anything green and fresh is a welcome accompaniment.

6 large eggs

4 cups milk (or for an incredibly delectable version, you can use part milk and part half-and-half, heavy [whipping] cream or crème fraîche)

2½ cups Chipotle-Cascabel Salsa (page 36)

½ cup chopped fresh cilantro

Salt, about 1 teaspoon

1 1-pound loaf crusty sourdough bread, cut into ¾-inch cubes, crust and all

2 cups (8 ounces) roughly chopped fully cooked smoked ham (optional)

¾ cup grated Parmesan cheese

I. In a large bowl, whisk the eggs until completely liquidy, then whisk in the milk, 2 *cups* of the salsa, the cilantro and salt. Stir in the bread, cover and let stand for 1 hour, pressing the bread down into the custard from time to time to ensure that it is soaking evenly. Stir in the ham if using.

2. Heat the oven to 350 degrees. Butter or oil a 13 x 9-inch baking dish, then scoop the bread pudding mixture into it. Splash the remaining ½ *cup* salsa over the top and sprinkle with the cheese. Bake until crusty and browned and just set in the middle, about 50 minutes. Let stand for several minutes before cutting into squares to serve.

Red Chile Pasta

. . . . .

Serves 8 as a pasta
course, 4 to 6 as a
main course

This is probably the easiest, most flexible recipe we've developed for this book. Though I like the way the richly flavored red chile salsa evenly coats the pasta strands, you can use whatever salsa appeals. The proportions I've used here are Italian in approach (light, flavorful), so my recommendation is to serve this dish as a separate course, before the main course. Search out real queso añejo *for a dish that may look Italian but will taste 100 percent Mexican (yes, dried pasta is eaten a lot in Mexico).*

2 cups Mellow Red Chile Salsa (page 30),
   at room temperature
1 tablespoon olive oil, preferably a
   delicious fruity one
2 cups coarsely chopped watercress leaves
   (no stems), plus a little more for garnish
   OR 1 cup chopped fresh cilantro, plus a
   little more for garnish
Salt to taste
1 pound dried linguine
¾ cup finely grated Mexican *queso añejo*,
   Parmesan or Romano

POSSIBLE ADD-INS:
1 cup lightly cooked young peas
1 cup flaked smoked fish, like white-
   fish, sable, trout or tuna
½ cup sour cream or crème fraîche
1½ cups shredded roasted or smoked
   chicken
⅔ cup crumbled cooked bacon
1 cup sautéed sliced mushrooms,
   preferably shiitakes or oysters

1. Put on a large pot of heavily salted water to boil—you'll need about 4 quarts to do this job well. Press the salsa through a medium-mesh strainer into a small saucepan to remove the skins. (If the salsa seems overly chunky, first give it a spin in the blender, then strain it.) Stir in the oil and the watercress or cilantro, and set over low heat to warm.

2. When the water is boiling, add the pasta; cook until tender but still resilient (what Italians call *al dente*), 8 to 10 minutes. Pour the pasta into a colander, shake off the excess water, then return it to the pot. Add the salsa mixture and any add-ins you've chosen and stir to coat the pasta well. Season with salt if necessary. Divide between warm plates, sprinkle with the cheese and a little watercress or cilantro, and serve right away.

Today's Macaroni and Cheese— it's not just for kids

Serves 8 generously

Okay, okay, I'll admit it. I grew up on macaroni and cheese. Not the cardboard-box-with-the-powdery-package version (though I learned to survive on that three-for-a-dollar variety during college). No, my family's macaroni and cheese was the slow-baked macaroni-milk-cheese version, and we featured it on my parents' restaurant menu every day for thirty-five years. Crusty cheese over submissive macaroni, and it was wonderful—at least to my youthful tongue. Here's another vision of that old childhood memory, this one developed by Deann. It's creamy, easy and, well, a little edgy.

2 cups milk
4 tablespoons (2 ounces) butter
¼ cup all-purpose flour
2 cups Roasted Poblano-Tomato Salsa or Roasted Jalapeño-Tomato Salsa (page 26 or 23)
3 cups (12 ounces) shredded Cheddar cheese

Salt, about 1½ teaspoons
1 pound dried pasta (though elbow macaroni will do, I suggest you try corkscrew cavatappi or the spiral rotini or fusilli)
About 2 tablespoons chopped fresh cilantro, for garnish

1. Into a large pot pour about 4 quarts of heavily salted water, cover and set over high heat. Measure the milk in a glass measuring cup and warm for a minute in a microwave on high (or warm in a small saucepan). In a medium-size saucepan, melt the butter over medium heat, then stir in the flour and whisk until the mixture turns deep gold, about 2 minutes. Add the warmed milk all at once and continue to whisk constantly until the mixture thickens and comes to a full boil, 4 to 5 minutes. (Whisk diligently and there will be no lumps.) Stir in the salsa, remove from the heat, then add the cheese and stir until it melts. Taste and season with salt.

2. When the water comes to a boil, add the dried pasta. Stir well so no pieces stick together and boil until the pasta is al dente, 8 to 10 minutes. Drain thoroughly and return to the pot. Stir in the cheese sauce, then spoon into a serving dish. Sprinkle with the cilantro and you're ready.

Note: For a pleasingly contrasting texture, spoon the macaroni and cheese into a buttered baking dish. Top with buttered bread crumbs and bake at 375 degrees until browned, 10 to 12 minutes.

Spicy Vegetable "Stew"

Serves 4

This smoky, spicy pot of vegetables and beans comes to my mind frequently when thinking about what to make for dinner. Thing is, for everyday meals, I like eating low on the food chain—grains, beans, legumes. It's healthier, more ecological and satisfying. Serve big spoonfuls of this "stew" alongside couscous or rice, and you've got a special dinner.

2 tablespoons olive or vegetable oil

1 medium-size white onion, diced, plus more for serving with the stew

2 small (about 12 ounces total) chayotes, cut into ½-inch dice (peel, seed and all)

2 cups Chipotle-Cascabel Salsa (page 36)

1 15-ounce can tomato sauce

3 tablespoons freshly ground corn *masa* for tortillas (you'll have to get this at a tortilla factory or well-stocked Mexican grocery) OR 3 tablespoons *masa harina*

Salt, about ½ teaspoon

1 medium (10 ounces) sweet potato, peeled and cut into ½-inch dice

1 15-ounce can garbanzo beans (chickpeas), drained

1 cup cooked black beans, drained

½ cup raisins or currants (optional)

2 cups green beans cut into 1-inch lengths or small broccoli florets, briefly blanched, or thawed if frozen

Generous ¼ cup chopped fresh cilantro

1. In a large saucepan, heat the oil over medium-high. Add the onion and chayotes and cook, stirring regularly, until richly browned, about 10 minutes.

2. Add the salsa, tomato sauce and 1 cup of water. Bring to a simmer, then reduce the heat to between medium and medium-low. In a small bowl, mix the fresh *masa* or *masa harina* with about 5 tablespoons of water, making sure there are no lumps. Hold a small strainer over the simmering pot and pour in the *masa*. As it dribbles into the pot, stir it thoroughly into the bubbling mixture. Press all of the *masa* through the strainer and into the pot. Stir until thickened, then taste and season with salt.

3. Add the sweet potato, partially cover the pot and simmer for 5 minutes. Add the garbanzo beans, black beans, and optional raisins and simmer for 5 minutes longer. Add the green beans or broccoli, let the stew return to a simmer, and you're ready to serve in warm deep bowls. Pass the cilantro, and extra onion if you want, for each guest to sprinkle on as he or she likes.

Toasty Fideos (Vermicelli) with Roasted Tomato, Black Beans and Chard

· · · · ·

Serves 4 generously as a main dish, 6 as a first course

Wait till you taste the toastiness of these noodles after they've been braised with roasted tomatoes, jalapeños, black beans and Swiss chard! Just as raw rice is browned before simmering for classic Mexican preparations, so are the popular dried vermicelli, the noodles sold as fideos all through Mexico (and the United States in Mexican groceries). Though fideos are typically browned in a deep skillet of oil, I've developed an easy method for oven-roasting oiled noodles; if you have an oil mister, use it here. The only meticulous step is stirring to completely separate the strands that make up the noodle nests. The most typical fideo preparation in Mexico is a brothy soup (kids' favorite); here we're offering it more in the "dry soup" version—"dry" because the noodles absorb most of the liquid, leaving them saucy rather than soupy.

2 cups Roasted Jalapeño-Tomato Salsa (page 23)
2 to 2¼ cups chicken or vegetable broth
About 1 teaspoon salt, depending on the saltiness of your broth
1 package (10 to 12 ounces) dried *fideo* (vermicelli) noodles, preferably the thinnest ones called "angel hair" and sold in nest shapes
About 1½ tablespoons vegetable or olive oil
2 cups cooked black beans, drained
1 bunch (about 8 good-size leaves) chard (look for red chard for the prettiest dish), stems removed, leaves sliced lengthwise in half, then crosswise into ½-inch strips
1½ cups (about 6 ounces) cubed Mexican *queso fresco* (½-inch cubes are good)
OR generous ½ cup finely grated Mexican *queso añejo*, Parmesan or Romano
⅓ cup chopped fresh cilantro

1. Heat the oven to 350 degrees. In a bowl, stir together the salsa, broth (the smaller amount for a 10-ounce package of *fideos,* the larger amount for a 12-ounce package) and salt.

2. Place the noodles in a 13 x 9-inch baking dish. Mist or brush both sides of the noodles thoroughly with the oil. Bake, turning the noodles over once, until golden brown on both sides, about 15 minutes. Pour the salsa mixture over the noodles, then turn all the noodles over again (this will ensure that they are all moistened). Cover with foil and bake for 10 minutes. Remove from the oven, uncover, stir the noodles to completely separate the strands (they should have softened enough for this) and stir in the beans and chard. (This is a little awkward—the pan will be full.) Re-cover and bake, stirring once, until the chard is cooked and the noodles are al dente, about 15 minutes.

3. Uncover, strew with the cheese and cilantro, and you're ready to carry this homey casserole to the table.

Chilaquiles (Tortilla Casserole) with spinach, zucchini and aged cheese

· · · · ·

Serves 4 generously as a main dish

Since Mexicans understand that the only good corn tortillas to serve with the meal have to be fresh, fresh, fresh—preferably still hot from the griddle—Mexican cooks have devised ingenious ways to use cold or stale leftover ones. A baked layered tortilla casserole (think lasagna) is popular, as are enchiladas and chilaquiles—a quick-simmered hodgepodge of crisp-fried tortilla chips, spicy sauce and vegetables, greens or meat. In Mexico it's a favorite brunch (almuerzo) dish. For the tortillas to come out tender but separate (not mushy) and lubricated with just the right amount of sauce, you'll have to choose the right ones. You can buy thick, good-quality eating tortillas and fry them in vegetable oil until crispy, or you can buy tortilla chips. Just remember, the best eating chips (thin, delicate and crispy) make the worst possible chilaquiles. Choose the thickest chips (preferably the homemade-looking ones at a Mexican grocery); measure by weight, not volume.

1 medium-size white onion, sliced

1 tablespoon vegetable oil

2 medium (10 ounces total) zucchini or other summer squash (look for different varieties at the farmers' market), cut into small dice

2 cups Roasty Red Guajillo Salsa (page 33)

2 cups rich-tasting chicken or vegetable broth, plus a little extra if necessary

½ teaspoon salt, plus a little more if necessary, depending on the saltiness of the broth

4 cups (about 5 ounces) stemmed spinach leaves, well rinsed

8 ounces (8 to 12 loosely packed cups, depending on the type) tortilla chips (thick ones that you make yourself or buy at a Mexican grocery are best)

About ½ cup finely grated Mexican *queso añejo*, Parmesan or Romano

1. In a large Dutch oven or flameproof casserole, cook the onion in the oil over medium-high until it begins to soften, about 5 minutes. Add the zucchini and cook, stirring frequently, until it begins to brown, about 3 minutes longer.

2. Add the salsa, 2 cups broth, the salt and spinach, bring to a boil, then stir in the chips, coating them with the broth mixture. When the mixture comes to a simmer, cover, remove from the heat and let stand for 5 minutes.

3. Very carefully stir the *chilaquiles* to check that the chips have softened nicely. I like them to still have a few chewy edges—though if there's too much crunch left, I dribble in a *little* extra broth and return them to the heat for a couple of minutes. Sprinkle with the cheese and they're ready to serve right from the vessel they were cooked in. Of course, you can spoon them onto warm plates in the kitchen before sprinkling each serving with the cheese. *Chilaquiles* should be served right away.

Seared Red-Chile Enchiladas with chicken and aged cheese

Serves 4

It's the bright, earthy red chile seared into the tortilla that I find so attractive in this kind of enchilada. I have since I was a kid. Even today, at the *taquería* inside my local Mexican grocery, my mouth waters when I see a plate of these enchiladas. The recipe here does not produce the saucy, cheesy enchiladas most of us know, but the kind I've enjoyed eating from street vendors all over Mexico. Simple, tender, spicy and, yes, a little oily—but that's half the fun. The result is a very Mexican-tasting casual meal. Because they require a little dexterity to produce, I offer the following tips for success: Have all the ingredients ready near the stove; have a light coating of oil in the pan or wok; heat it hot enough to sear and brown the tortilla in 8 to 10 seconds (if it takes longer, the tortillas will soften so much that they'll fall apart); and start frying the enchiladas when you're ready to serve them. Even if your first attempts don't look beautiful, they'll taste fabulous.

4 small (about 8 ounces total) boiling potatoes (like the red-skinned ones), scrubbed and cut into ¼-inch dice

1½ cups Mellow Red Chile Salsa (page 30)

1½ tablespoons cider vinegar

1½ teaspoons dried oregano, preferably Mexican

¾ teaspoon black pepper, preferably freshly ground

Scant ½ teaspoon cumin, preferably freshly ground

Salt, about ¾ teaspoon, plus a little more for the chicken

About 4 tablespoons vegetable oil

1 small white onion, thinly sliced

1½ cups (loosely packed) coarsely shredded cooked chicken (I'd either poach, grill or broil a large whole chicken breast or buy a small rotisserie chicken to shred)

8 corn tortillas, preferably store-bought

About ⅓ cup finely grated Mexican *queso añejo*, Parmesan or Romano

About ½ cup fresh cilantro leaves

1. In a small saucepan, boil the potatoes in salted water until tender, about 10 minutes; drain thoroughly and pat dry. In a blender, puree the salsa with the vinegar, oregano, black pepper and cumin. Taste and season with salt (the salsa should taste somewhat salty). Pour it into a pie plate and set it near your stove.

2. In a large skillet (I prefer one that is 12 inches and nonstick) or wok, heat 1 *tablespoon* of the oil over medium-high. Add the onion and drained potatoes and stir-fry until the potatoes are richly browned and the onion is crisp-tender, about 5 minutes. Stir in 2 tablespoons of the salsa mixture, cook for another minute, then scrape into a heatproof bowl. Cover with foil and keep warm in the oven. Heat the chicken over low with ⅓ cup of the salsa mixture and salt, cover and keep warm.

3. Wipe out the skillet or wok, add 1 *tablespoon* more of the oil and set over medium-high heat. Dip both sides of 2 tortillas into the sauce. (They should be coated with a medium-thick layer of sauce—too little and they'll be tasteless, too thick and the sauce will be gloppy.) Lay the coated tortillas in the hot oil. Cook for 8 to 10 seconds, then flip the tortillas with a metal spatula. Immediately lay about 2 tablespoons of the chicken on each tortilla, and, after cooking a few seconds longer, fold them in half to enclose the chicken. (The tortillas should look seared—deliciously browned in spots—but not be crispy.) Lift them out, draining as much oil as possible back into the pan and lay them slightly overlapping on a warm dinner plate. Keep warm in the oven. Repeat with the rest of the tortillas, adding oil as needed (be sure to let it heat sufficiently) and arranging each pair on another warm dinner plate.

4. Spoon a quarter of the potato mixture over each serving and sprinkle liberally with the cheese and cilantro leaves. Serve without hesitation.

Layered Tortilla "Lasagna" with greens and cheese

Serves 8 as a main dish, 12 to 16 as an accompaniment

A square of this cheesy, full-of-vegetables tortilla casserole is welcome at any informal gathering, lunch or supper. It possesses flavors and textures that draw you back time and again. If the frying of the tortillas is something you like to avoid, steam them as directed on page 87, then layer the dish, bake it and eat it right away. The texture will be a little more like pudding, since the unfried tortillas will soak up a considerable amount of sauce. In Mexico, these homey casseroles are a way to use up stale corn tortillas; they are typically called budín de tortilla, budín azteca or tamal azteca.

About 4 tablespoons vegetable oil

3 cups (about 6 ounces) sliced stemmed mushrooms (this is delicious with really flavorful mushrooms like shiitakes)

1½ cups corn kernels, preferably freshly cut off the cobs (you'll need about 2 ears)

8 cups (about 10 ounces) packed stemmed spinach leaves, well rinsed but not dried

½ teaspoon salt

16 tortillas (this is better with store-bought tortillas rather than homemade)

5 cups Chipotle-Cascabel Salsa (page 36)

1 cup heavy (whipping) cream, crème fraîche or plain yogurt

3 cups (12 ounces) shredded Mexican Chihuahua cheese, brick, Monterey Jack or just about any melting cheese you like

1 15- or 16-ounce carton ricotta cheese

About ⅓ cup chopped fresh cilantro, for garnish

1. Heat *1 tablespoon* of the oil in a large skillet over medium. When quite hot, add the mushrooms and cook, stirring, until just tender, 3 to 5 minutes. Add the corn and cook for a minute or two longer, then scrape the mixture into a bowl. Return the skillet to the heat without washing it and add the damp spinach. Cook, stirring constantly, until just wilted, 2 to 3 minutes. Scoop into a colander set in the sink and use a spoon to gently press out excess moisture. Let the vegetables cool, then scoop the spinach in with the mushrooms and corn and season with the salt.

2. Pour *a little* of the remaining oil into a small skillet to lightly coat the bottom and set over medium heat until hot. One at a time, quick-fry the tortillas for a few seconds per side just to soften them. As the oil is used up, add a little more, let it heat a moment, then continue frying tortillas. Drain the tortillas in a single layer on paper towels, blotting them dry with additional towels. Cut the tortillas in half.

3. Heat the oven to 350 degrees. Lightly oil a 13 x 9-inch baking dish. In a medium-size bowl, mix the salsa with the cream or yogurt. Spread a thin layer of the salsa mixture over the bottom of the baking dish, then cover with 8 tortilla halves. Evenly top with half of the vegetables, a scant 1½ cups of the remaining salsa mixture and *1 cup* of the shredded cheese. Add another layer of 8 tortilla halves. Spread with the ricotta and another scant 1½ cups of the salsa mixture. Top that second layer with a third round of 8 tortilla halves, the remaining vegetables, another portion of salsa mixture and *1 cup* of the shredded cheese. For the final layer, evenly lay out the remaining tortillas, spread with the remaining salsa mixture (making sure to completely cover the tortillas) and evenly sprinkle on the remaining *1 cup* shredded cheese.

4. Cover lightly with foil and bake for 25 minutes. Uncover and bake for an additional 10 to 15 minutes, until bubbling and lightly browned. Let stand a few minutes before sprinkling with the cilantro and cutting into squares to serve to your guests on warm plates.

POULTRY, MEAT AND FISH MAIN COURSES

CHILE-GLAZED ROAST CHICKEN • TOMATILLO-BAKED CHICKEN BREASTS WITH ROASTED ASPARAGUS • SOFT TACOS OF GRILLED CHICKEN BREAST WITH TANGY GREEN CHILE AND GRILLED ONIONS • BURNISHED CORNISH HENS WITH ROASTED ONIONS AND SWEET POTATOES • SLOW-GRILLED TURKEY BREAST (OR LAMB LEG) WITH MEDITERRANEAN SALSA • ROBUST BEEF BRISKET WITH RED CHILE AND WINTER VEGETABLES • PEPPERY PAN-SEARED STEAKS WITH SMOKY *CREMA* AND BLUE CHEESE • CHORIZO AND BLACK BEAN CHILI • SPICY JALAPEÑO BEEF TIPS • TOMATILLO-BRAISED PORK LOIN WITH HERBY WHITE BEANS AND BACON • GRILLED-AND-GLAZED PORK TENDERLOIN WITH MUSTARDY SWEET ONIONS • SMOKY GLAZED HAM FOR A CROWD • GUAJILLO-SPIKED SHELLFISH SOUP • RED CHILE RICE WITH SHRIMP AND BACON • SEARED SEA SCALLOPS WITH JALAPEÑO CREAM • GREEN CHILE CRAB CAKES • RED-GLAZED WHOLE FISH • POBLANO-BAKED FISH FILLETS

Chile-Glazed Roast Chicken

Serves 4

I think you'll feel triumphant carrying this lustrous bird from oven to table, perfuming the air with captivating aromas. And why not make two while you're at it? The second involves scarcely more work, and the leftovers are wonderful shredded into pasta or sliced for sandwiches with a little mayonnaise and extra salsa. In the summer I cook it in a closed kettle grill over a drip pan, coals banked to the sides. If a whole bird is not for you, substitute six bone-in chicken breast halves, and cook for 25 to 30 minutes.

1 whole chicken, about 3¼ pounds
2 cups Chipotle-Cascabel Salsa (page 36)
1 tablespoon olive or vegetable oil

2 tablespoons honey
Watercress, flat-leaf parsley or fresh cilantro sprigs, for garnish

1. Rinse the chicken, pat dry with paper towels and place in a non-aluminum pan or in a large plastic food bag. Spoon on (or measure in) *half* of the salsa and turn the chicken to coat it thoroughly. Refrigerate for at least 1 hour or as long as overnight.

2. Heat the oven to 375 degrees. Remove the chicken from the marinade and place it in a roasting pan; reserve the marinade that's left behind. Brush the chicken with the oil, set it in the oven and roast for 45 minutes. Mix the honey with the reserved marinade and drizzle it over the chicken. Return to the oven and roast until the juices run clear when the thigh is pierced deeply with a fork (an instant-read thermometer should register about 170 degrees when inserted at the thickest part of the thigh), about 15 minutes more. If the chicken browns quickly, loosely cover it with foil during the last few minutes of roasting.

3. Use a large fork and a spatula to help you transfer the chicken to a plate. Loosely tent with foil and let stand while you prepare the sauce. Spoon the rendered fat off the juices that have collected in the pan, then stir in the remaining *1 cup* salsa. Set over medium heat and stir, dislodging all the delicious browned bits in the pan, as the salsa comes to a simmer. Scrape the warm salsa into a sauce dish. Carve the chicken and arrange it on a warm serving platter. Garnish with the watercress, parsley or cilantro and you're ready to serve, passing the sauce separately for each guest to spoon on.

Tomatillo-Baked Chicken Breasts with roasted asparagus

· · · · ·

Serves 6

With tomatillo salsa in the pantry (or refrigerator or freezer), in just minutes you can produce an impressive meal of thoroughly charming classic flavors—tangy tomatillo softened with thick cream, smothering tender chicken. The roasted asparagus is a delicious, if untraditional, accompaniment. And when it's not in season, try roasted green beans (I steam them for 2 minutes first and roast them a little less) or simply roasted potatoes or parsnips.

2 medium-size bunches (about 1½ pounds total) asparagus, ends trimmed, lower stalks peeled if they seem tough
2 tablespoons olive oil
6 large (about 2½ pounds total) boneless, skinless chicken breast halves

½ cup heavy (whipping) cream or crème fraîche
2 cups Roasted Tomatillo Salsa (page 28)
⅓ cup chopped fresh cilantro

I. Heat the oven to 400 degrees. Lay the asparagus on a large baking sheet, drizzle with the oil and sprinkle with a little salt. Toss to coat the asparagus evenly.

2. Lightly oil a 13 x 9-inch baking dish, then lay in the chicken breasts. In a bowl, mix together the cream and tomatillo salsa. Spoon it over the chicken, set it in the oven and bake for 10 minutes. Set the baking sheet of asparagus in the oven and bake everything about 15 minutes longer, until the asparagus is browned and crunchy-tender (turn the spears once or twice during baking) and the chicken has lost all but the faintest hint of pink at the center.

3. Arrange a portion of the asparagus on each of 6 warm dinner plates and lay a chicken breast over each portion. Stir the sauce that's still in the pan to bring it together. (If the chicken has exuded a lot of juice, pour the sauce into a pan and cook it down over high heat to the consistency of cream soup.) Taste and season with a little extra salt if you think it needs it, then spoon the sauce over the chicken breasts, letting it run down on the asparagus. Sprinkle with chopped cilantro and you're ready to serve.

Soft Tacos of Grilled Chicken Breast with tangy green chile and grilled onions

• • • • •

Makes 8 moderate servings

Anyone who's experienced the enticing allure of spicy grilled chicken from a street stall in Mexico will understand what this dish is all about. Lip-tingling seared chicken (here chicken breasts) dressed out with Roasted Poblano-Tomato Salsa and lime is served wrapped in soft, steamy tortillas with grilled green onions. These are some of the most classic flavors from Mexico, and they're perfect for summer entertaining. Start your guests with some Tangy Green Guacamole (page 40) and accompany your tacos with a big salad or bowls of pinto beans simmered with bacon and roasted tomato. Frontera's Chocolate Pecan Pie Bars (page 112) or Paletas Mexicanas (page 118) would give just the right finish.

2 to 4 fresh jalapeño chiles, stems removed (optional but desirable for those who like it spicy)

2 cups Roasted Poblano-Tomato Salsa (page 26), plus more if you've got a salsa-hungry crowd

1 tablespoon Worcestershire sauce

3 limes, each cut into 6 wedges

8 large (about 3½ pounds total) boneless chicken breast halves

18 green onions, roots and wilted greens removed

A few tablespoons vegetable or olive oil

2 to 3 dozen steaming-hot corn tortillas (see Note page 87)

1. In a small ungreased skillet, dry-roast the jalapeños over medium heat, turning them regularly, until the chiles are soft and well darkened in spots, 5 to 10 minutes. Place in a food processor or blender with ¾ cup of the salsa, the Worcestershire and the juice from 3 or 4 lime wedges. Process to a smooth puree. Arrange the chicken breasts in a single layer in a baking dish, pour the salsa mixture over them, cover and refrigerate for at least 1 hour but not more than overnight.

2. Preheat a gas grill or light a charcoal fire and let burn until the coals are covered with gray ash. With a brush (or an oil mister), lightly coat the green onions with oil, then lay them over the fire in a spot that's not too hot. Grill, turning them regularly, until they're soft, sweet and

mouthwateringly browned, about 4 minutes. Remove 2 of the largest green onions, chop them into ¼-inch pieces and stir into the remaining *1¼ cups* of salsa. Squeeze another lime wedge or two over the remaining onions and keep them warm on the side of the grill or in a low oven.

3. Remove the chicken breasts from the marinade, scraping as much as possible back into the pan; reserve the marinade. Brush (or mist) the chicken lightly on both sides with oil, lay on well-oiled hot grill grates and grill until cooked through but still juicy, about 8 minutes per side. During the last couple of minutes on the grill, brush a nice coating of the reserved marinade over the chicken.

4. Slice the chicken into ½-inch-wide strips, scoop it onto a warm serving platter and flank with the grilled onions and lime wedges. Pass the platter with hot tortillas kept warm in a towel-lined basket. Let your guests make their own soft tacos of the chicken and grilled onions, encouraging them to spoon on the salsa-onion mixture and squeeze on lime to their liking.

Note: In *Rick Bayless's Mexican Kitchen,* we described a good method for heating corn tortillas: Wrap them by the dozen in clean kitchen towels, lay the packages in a single layer in a steamer, set the lid in place, bring the water to a strong boil for 1 minute, then remove from the heat and let stand, covered, for 15 minutes. For larger quantities, as called for in this recipe, you may find the following easier: Set a cooling rack over a roasting pan containing about 1 inch of simmering water; lay the tortillas a few at a time on the rack and steam them until thoroughly soft. Stack them by the dozen, wrap in towels and keep warm in a small ice chest (without ice of course) or similar insulated container. You may also heat the corn tortillas in the microwave (wrapped in microwave-grade plastic wrap in stacks of 10 to 12) for 1 minute on high before storing them in an insulated container, though they don't tend to be quite as freshly moist.

Burnished Cornish Hens with roasted onions and sweet potatoes

Serves 4

These saucy little birds make an impression. Mellow red chile naps a whole, ultratender fowl for each guest, puddling down around tender sweet potatoes to create a fabulous combination of flavors. If you shop at a Mexican grocery, look for the native sweet potato that'll be sold as camote morado—purple on the outside, white inside, with a taste that's creamy and wonderfully sweet. The high-heat roasting technique we've employed here translates into limited time expended and very moist results. If the hens don't brown to your liking, run them under a broiler for a minute or so for more color.

4 Cornish game hens, each about 1¼ pounds
2½ cups Mellow Red Chile Salsa (page 30)
2 large (about 1½ pounds total) sweet potatoes or Mexican *camote* (the purple-skinned, white-fleshed sweet potatoes), peeled and cut into 1-inch cubes
1 large white onion, cut into ⅜-inch-thick slices

½ cup fresh orange juice
About 2 tablespoons olive or vegetable oil
Salt, preferably coarse, kosher type
1 generous teaspoon chopped fresh thyme, plus sprigs for garnish
1 tablespoon orange liqueur (optional)

1. Rinse the hens, pat dry, place in a large bowl or large plastic food bag and drizzle with the salsa. Turn to coat them well. Cover and let stand at room temperature for 1 hour or refrigerate as long as overnight.

2. In a large saucepan, bring to a boil several inches of heavily salted water. Add the sweet potatoes and boil for 5 minutes. Add the onion and cook for 3 minutes longer, until both are *nearly* tender (the sweet potatoes can still have a slight crunch at the center). Drain and spread on a tray to cool.

3. Heat the oven to 450 degrees. Remove the hens from the marinade, scraping as much marinade as possible back into the bowl. Stir the orange juice into the marinade.

4. Lightly oil a large roasting pan and place the birds in it, breast side up and legs facing out. Brush the hens with oil and sprinkle liberally with salt. Roast for 20 minutes. Remove the pan from the oven and scatter the potatoes, onions and fresh thyme around the hens. Spoon all of the marinade mixture over the hens and vegetables and return to the oven. Roast until the hens' juices run clear when the thighs are pierced with a knife, about 15 minutes more.

5. With a pair of tongs, remove the hens and vegetables to a large serving platter and loosely cover with foil. Spoon off the fat from the pan juices, then place the roasting pan over medium heat and boil, scraping up any browned bits from the bottom of the pan, until reduced to a light cream sauce consistency. Taste and season with the liqueur if using and salt if necessary. Spoon the sauce around the hens and vegetables, decorate the platter with sprigs of thyme, and you're ready to present your beautiful creation.

Slow-Grilled Turkey Breast (or Lamb Leg) with Mediterranean Salsa

Serves 8

Cooking boneless turkey breast or lamb leg by the "indirect" method in a kettle grill is just about the nicest thing you can do to either one. The moist, smoky heat cooks gently, meaning the meat will cook to the doneness you like without drying out. Though a charcoal grill is my preference, a gas one may be employed here by heating only the burners on the edges of the grill, leaving those directly under the meat turned off; since no drip pan is used, replace the drippings with water. You may be amazed how a salsa that tastes quintessentially Mexican can be so easily transformed into flavors that evoke North Africa. Chiles are, after all, the thread that weaves through the cooking of all warm-weather cuisines. Here, enlivened with apricots and olives, the tangy guajillo salsa shows a new and beautiful face.

2 cups Roasty Red Guajillo Salsa (page 33)
3 tablespoons Worcestershire sauce
2 tablespoons balsamic vinegar
1 whole (about 3 pounds) boneless turkey breast, skin still on and split into two halves
    OR 1 butterflied (about 3 pounds) boneless leg of lamb
½ cup chopped dried apricots, tossed with a little hot water to soften

½ cup chopped pitted black olives, preferably the wrinkly oil-cured kind
2 tablespoons chopped fresh parsley, plus a few sprigs for garnish
2 teaspoons finely chopped lemon zest (colored peel only), plus a few thin strips for garnish

1. Mix together *1 cup* of the salsa with 2 *tablespoons* of the Worcestershire and the vinegar. Place the turkey or lamb in a large dish, smear both sides completely with the salsa mixture, cover and refrigerate for several hours or as long as overnight.

2. About half an hour before cooking, prepare a charcoal fire in a kettle-style grill, letting the coals burn until they are covered with gray ash. Bank the coals on two sides of the lower grate, then set a 12 x 9-inch aluminum-foil pan (or something similar) on the grate in between the two piles of coals. Pour about ½ inch of water into the pan. Set the cooking grate in place.

3. Remove the turkey or lamb from the pan (discard leftover marinade) and position it on the cooking grate over the drip pan. Set the grill cover in place. Let cook for about 50 minutes, checking two or three times to ensure that the meat is moving along nicely—roasting and smoking and caramelizing to a glossy mahogany brown. Check for doneness: the turkey should reach an internal temperature of about 160 degrees on a meat or instant-read thermometer, the lamb should reach 135 to 140 degrees. If you don't have a thermometer, cut into the turkey or lamb at the thickest part to ensure that it's as done as you like—the turkey should not have more than a trace of pink and the juices should run clear. Remove from the grill to a rack set in a roasting pan, cover with foil and set in a low oven while you're finishing the preparations.

4. Carefully remove the grill grate and then the drip pan. Tip the pan and spoon off all the fat that you can. Spoon ¼ cup of the degreased drippings into a small bowl. Stir in the remaining *1 cup* salsa, the remaining *1 tablespoon* Worcestershire, the apricots, olives, parsley and lemon zest. The mixture should be an easily spoonable "salsa" consistency; if it's too thick, stir in another tablespoon of the drippings.

5. Slice the turkey or lamb and lay on a warm serving platter. Decorate with sprigs of parsley and strips of lemon zest. You're ready to serve your guests, passing the salsa separately.

Robust Beef Brisket with red chile and winter vegetables

Serves 8

When the January windows are shut tight, nothing smells as warming as a long-braising brisket in the oven. The hours of gentle heat render this otherwise tough cut a fork-tender prize and the gentle glow of red chile makes my spirit, at least, fortified for any kind of weather.

1 beef brisket (choose the flat end if possible; it'll be about 4 pounds), trimmed of most surface fat

2 large garlic cloves, peeled and quartered

Salt, about 2 teaspoons

6 large carrots, peeled and cut into 2-inch pieces

4 large (about 2½ pounds total) baking (Idaho, russet) potatoes, peeled and cut lengthwise in 4 wedges

3 large red or white onions, each cut into 6 wedges

2 cups Mellow Red Chile Salsa (page 30)

2 bunches watercress or a handful of flat-leaf parsley sprigs, for garnish

1. Heat the oven to 425 degrees. Lay the brisket in a lightly oiled roasting pan large enough to hold it *and* all the vegetables in a single layer. Thoroughly rub both sides of the brisket with the cut side of the garlic cloves, then make small slits in the meat and insert the garlic pieces into the slits. Sprinkle both sides generously with some of the salt and turn the brisket fat side up. Roast until the top is nicely browned, about 30 minutes. Carefully turn it over, return it to the oven and brown the other side, about 20 minutes more. Remove from the oven and reduce the oven temperature to 350 degrees.

2. Surround the brisket with the carrots, potatoes and onions, then sprinkle them with about ½ *teaspoon* of the salt. In a small bowl, combine the salsa with 1½ cups water and drizzle the mixture over everything in the pan, being careful to completely cover the vegetables. Cover the pan tightly with foil and bake until the meat and vegetables are both very tender, about 2

hours. Remove from the oven and let stand for 15 to 20 minutes for the meat to absorb as much of the juices as possible.

3. Using 2 large forks or spatulas, transfer the meat to a cutting board. Thinly slice the meat across the grain (it's obvious if you start in the wrong direction; the slices will look as if they're made up of long strands). Arrange the slices in the center of a warm serving platter and surround them with the vegetables. Lightly cover with foil while you finish the sauce: Tip the roasting pan to collect the juices in one end and spoon off most of the fat. Set the pan over medium-high heat and stir nearly constantly until the juices are boiled down to a light saucy (no longer juicy) consistency. Taste and season with salt if you think it needs a little, then spoon the sauce over the meat and vegetables. Garnish the platter with the watercress or parsley and set before your guests.

Peppery Pan-Seared Steaks with *smoky crema and blue cheese*

· · · · ·

Serves 4 heartily

These up-to-date–flavored steaks make a stellar center-piece for a very special occasion. When the weather's not right for firing up the grill, marinate some really good steaks with smoky chipotle salsa, pan-sear them as I've described here, then make a simple spicy sauce of the salsa, cream and blue cheese right in the pan you've used for cooking the steaks. The result will taste like you're on a live-it-up vacation. This recipe is a perfect example of how the earthy, elemental flavors of Mexico easily transcend the traditional kitchen, working their vibrant magic on dishes from practically anywhere.

1 cup Chipotle-Cascabel Salsa (page 36)
2 teaspoons freshly and rather coarsely ground black pepper
4 good-size 1-inch-thick steaks, size to suit your budget or preference (for a rustic dinner, I'd choose T-bones; for a dressier one, rib-eyes, strip steaks or tenderloins)

1 to 2 tablespoons olive or vegetable oil
1 medium-size red onion, thinly sliced
⅓ cup heavy (whipping) cream
½ cup crumbled blue cheese
A couple of tablespoons chopped fresh parsley, for garnish

1. In a blender, process the salsa until very smooth. Measure out 3 *tablespoons* of the salsa, stir in the black pepper, then smear this mixture over both sides of the steaks. Cover and refriger-ate for at least an hour or as long as overnight.

2. Turn the oven on to its lowest setting. With an exhaust fan on, heat a large heavy skillet (or use 2 skillets) over medium for 7 or 8 minutes (this works best with cast iron if you have it). Add the oil, swirl it in the pan, then lay in the steaks. Cook for 3 or 4 minutes until crusty on one side. Flip the steaks over and cook on the other side until they're done to your liking. A 1-inch-thick rib-eye steak will be cooked to medium-rare in 4 to 5 minutes after you've flipped it. Remove to a rack set over a plate and keep warm in the oven.

3. With the skillet still over the heat, add the onion and cook, stirring nearly constantly, until lightly browned but still crunchy, about 5 minutes. Stir in the remaining salsa and the cream and bring to a simmer. Add the blue cheese and stir until the cheese melts. Add any juices that may have accumulated under the steaks, then taste the sauce and add a little salt if you think it needs it.

4. Set a steak on each of 4 warm dinner plates, spoon a little sauce over each one, then sprinkle with chopped parsley. Your steaks are ready to eat.

Chorizo and Black Bean Chili

Serves 4 to 6
as a main dish

When the event is "Chili Making," I'm a purist, starting with hand-cut cubes of beef and pork, whole ancho chile pods and toasted, fresh-ground spices. It's traditional and it takes the better part of the day. But when I'm looking for a satisfying cup of something easy to serve to spirited friends, this modern-tasting chorizo and black bean braise is the ticket. If raw Mexican chorizo is unavailable, use coarsely ground beef, pork or turkey; with those choices add some crushed red pepper flakes and a touch of vinegar to help make up for missing flavors.

1 medium-size red onion, chopped
1 bunch green onions, roots trimmed off, cut into ¼-inch pieces
4 garlic cloves, finely chopped
1 pound raw Mexican chorizo sausage, casing removed
2 cups Roasty Red Guajillo Salsa (page 33)
3½ cups cooked black beans, drained
2 15-ounce cans diced tomatoes, undrained

1 teaspoon dried oregano, preferably Mexican
1 cup shredded Mexican Chihuahua cheese, brick, Monterey Jack or Cheddar, for garnish
½ cup chopped fresh cilantro, for garnish
½ cup sour cream, for garnish (optional)

1. Mix the red onion, *half* of the green onions, the garlic and chorizo in a large saucepan and set over medium heat. Cook, stirring from time to time, until the onions are soft and the chorizo cooked through, about 15 minutes. Raise the heat to medium-high and cook, stirring, until everything is richly browned. Spoon the mixture onto a plate lined with paper towels to drain off the fat. Stir the salsa and ½ cup of water into the pan, scraping the bottom of the pan to incorporate the browned bits. Add the beans, tomatoes, oregano and drained chorizo mixture. Partially cover, reduce the heat to medium-low and simmer for 30 to 45 minutes to blend the flavors.

2. Set out the garnishes in small bowls: the remaining green onions, the cheese, cilantro and the optional sour cream. Serve the chili in warm bowls and pass the garnishes separately for each guest to add to his or her liking.

Tomatillo-Braised Pork Loin with
herby white beans and bacon (page 98)

Guajillo-Spiked Shellfish Soup (page 104)

Red Chile Rice with Shrimp and Bacon (page 105)

Seared Sea Scallops with Jalapeño Cream (page 106)

Red-Glazed Whole Fish (page 108)

Frontera's Chocolate Pecan Pie Bars (page 112)

Paletas Mexicanas (Mexican Fruit Pops) (page 118)

Tequila with Sangrita—traditional spicy tequila chaser (page 119)

Spicy Jalapeño Beef Tips

Serves 4

This is about the simplest, most typical-tasting everyday dish in Mexican eateries from Tijuana to Tulum—chunks of beef seared quickly in a hot skillet, with tomatoes, jalapeño chiles, onions and garlic. Weave in a little red wine or Worcestershire, as I have suggested here, and you have a most memorable meal that didn't take all afternoon to make.

2 tablespoons bacon drippings, rich-tasting pork lard or olive oil

1¼ pounds tender boneless beef (sirloin, strip steak, rib-eye or tenderloin), cut into 1-inch cubes and patted dry

Salt, a liberal sprinkling for the meat, plus a little for the sauce if necessary

1 large white onion, thinly sliced

⅓ cup red wine
OR 1 tablespoon Worcestershire sauce

1 15-ounce can diced tomatoes, drained

2 cups Roasted Jalapeño-Tomato Salsa (page 23)

½ to ¾ cup sliced pickled jalapeños, well drained (optional)

⅓ cup chopped fresh cilantro, plus a few sprigs for garnish
OR a couple of tablespoons chopped fresh *epazote*, plus a few leaves or sprigs for garnish

1. In a large heavy skillet, heat the bacon drippings, lard or oil over medium-high. Sprinkle the meat liberally with salt. When the fat is quite hot, lay in the meat cubes in an uncrowded layer and quick-fry, stirring and turning them all regularly, until nicely browned, 4 to 5 minutes. Remove with a slotted spoon to a plate. (If you cut into a cube of meat, it should be cooked no more than about medium-rare.)

2. With the skillet still on the heat, add the onion and cook, stirring, for 4 or 5 minutes until golden, then add the wine or Worcestershire and stir as it quickly evaporates. Next add the tomatoes and stir regularly for 2 to 3 minutes as they darken and any liquid they lose evaporates (this will sweeten them considerably). Lastly add the salsa, optional pickled jalapeños and whichever herb you've chosen. Bring to a simmer, then reduce the heat to medium. Taste the sauce and season with salt if necessary.

3. Return the meat to the pan along with any juice that has accumulated on the plate. Heat through or simmer for a couple of minutes if you like your meat more done, then spoon onto a warm platter and garnish with herb sprigs. Dinner is ready.

Tomatillo-Braised Pork Loin with herby white beans and bacon

Serves 4 to 6

This is one of the best dishes we've included in this book. And though you'll think "Italian" when you lay the slices of roast pork alongside the saucy white beans, one bite will convince you that Mexico gave this dish its soul. With salsa at the ready, everything about this spectacular dish is quite simple, so keep this recipe in mind when you're entertaining without a lot of time to spare. (You could even use rinsed canned white beans to save time.) If you see fresh purslane (verdolagas) at the farmers' market or have it growing in your garden, add young 2-inch pieces to the sauce along with the beans for a traditionally Mexican flavor.

1 cup (7 ounces) small dried white beans, picked over

1 teaspoon mixed dried herbs (thyme and marjoram are classic in Mexico)

3 bay leaves

4 thick slices smoky bacon

1 2-pound boneless pork loin roast, untied

Salt, about 1 teaspoon, plus a sprinkling for the sauce and meat

3 cups Roasted Tomatillo Salsa (page 28)

1 small branch fresh *epazote* if available

Sprigs of cilantro, parsley, watercress or *epazote,* for garnish

I. In a medium-size saucepan, combine the beans with 3 cups of water and add the herbs and bay leaves. Partially cover the pan and bring to a good rolling boil over high heat. Reduce the heat to medium-low and simmer the beans very gently (still partially covered) until they are tender, about 1 hour (if you simmer them gently enough, they won't begin to fall apart before becoming thoroughly tender). Add more water if the beans ever begin peeking up above the surface of the water.

2. While the beans cook, in a 6-quart Dutch oven cook the bacon slices over medium heat, turning them occasionally, until thoroughly crispy. Remove to drain on paper towels, and when cool, crumble. Tip the Dutch oven slightly, spoon off most of the fat that collects, and add it to the simmering beans.

3. Heat the oven to 325 degrees. If your pork loin roast is in two sections that have been tied together, untie them. Sprinkle the meat liberally with salt. Heat the Dutch oven over medium-high until quite hot. Lay in the pork and brown thoroughly on all sides, about 10 minutes total. Pour in the salsa and nestle in the *epazote* if you have it. Cover the pot and place it in the oven. Cook until the pork registers about 150 degrees on a meat or instant-read thermometer; the meat will feel rather firm (not hard) to the touch, and cutting into the center will reveal only the slightest hint of pink. The total cooking time should be about 40 minutes. Remove the *epazote* and set the pot aside uncovered.

4. When the beans are tender, season them with about 1 teaspoon salt, let stand for a few minutes for the beans to absorb the seasoning, then drain off their cooking liquid. Remove the pork to a cutting board, add the beans to the pork pot, set over medium heat and season with salt. Slice the pork, laying the slices slightly overlapping on a warm serving platter. Spoon the beans and sauce around the meat, sprinkle everything with the crumbled bacon, garnish with herb sprigs and carry to the table.

Grilled-and-Glazed Pork Tenderloin with mustardy sweet onions

- - - - -

Serves 6 generously

Though pork with mustard is an established classic, spinning in some zesty salsa and the crunchy sweetness of grilled onions made me look at the combination with new hungry eyes. To learn to test the doneness of pork by touching, fold your thumb into the center of your palm, then wrap your fingers around your thumb, grasping it firmly. Now, with the forefinger of your other hand, press lightly and repeatedly on that bulging nugget of muscle at the base of your thumb. When you clench your fist with as much strength as you can muster, that little bit of muscle will become very firm, feeling like overcooked pork. Relax a little bit (keeping a fist), and you'll feel what deliciously cooked pork should feel like. Relax your fist completely while keeping it in the same position, and you'll experience what raw pork feels like.

⅓ cup spicy brown or Dijon-style mustard
1½ cups Roasted Poblano-Tomato Salsa
   (page 26)
4 large red onions, cut into ¼-inch-thick
   slices
3 large (about 2¼ pounds total) pork tenderloins, trimmed of fat and whitish "silverskin," cut crosswise in half (making 6 6-ounce portions)

About 2 tablespoons olive oil
Salt and freshly ground black pepper
Watercress or flat-leaf parsley sprigs,
   for garnish

1. In a small bowl, mix together the mustard and *⅓ cup* of the salsa.

2. Preheat a gas grill to medium or light a charcoal fire and let burn until the charcoal is covered with a thin layer of gray ash. Lay the onion slices in a single layer on one end of a large baking sheet, the pork on the other end. Brush with the olive oil (this is the place to use an oil mister if you have one) and sprinkle with salt and pepper. Carefully turn everything over and oil and season the other side.

3. Lay the pork in the center of the grill (this should be the hottest spot) and the onion slices in a single layer around the cooler edges of the grill. (If the onions and pork don't fit on your grill at the same time, cook the onions first and keep them warm in a low oven while you grill the pork.) Cover and cook for 10 minutes, until the pork is nicely browned underneath and the onions are softening. Turn the pork and onions over (with the onions now softening, the rings likely won't stay together—that's okay). Baste the pork and onions liberally with the mustard glaze. Re-cover the grill and cook until the pork is just done (it should read 150 degrees on a meat or instant-read thermometer and feel *nearly* firm when touched) and the onions are very soft, 10 to 15 minutes.

4. Use a pair of tongs to transfer the onions to a warm serving platter and drizzle with another *couple tablespoons* of the remaining salsa. Arrange the pork over the onions, decorate with the watercress or parsley and you're ready to serve this platter of delicious simplicity with the remaining salsa to pass separately for your guests to drizzle on to their own liking.

Smoky Glazed Ham for a Crowd

The caramel crunch of this ham's smoky crust may remind you of the honey-baked variety, but the flavor is all Spice Girls meet Gypsy Kings. And just imagine the smoky-spicy nuttiness of Chipotle-Cascabel Salsa turned into the perfect, modern-day, tangy-fruity ham condiment—this is great food for a crowd. You'll need a good ham to make this; I go to a local butcher shop (there are still a few around) and buy a house-smoked ham with no water added. If you don't have a small blowtorch to do the browning, you can use your broiler, though I'll warn you that the browning won't be nearly as uniform.

1 12- to 16-pound fully cooked smoked bone-in ham (look for one with no water added)

3 cups Chipotle-Cascabel Salsa (page 36)

About 3 tablespoons vegetable or olive oil

½ cup sugar

1 medium-size white onion, diced

1 cup coarsely pureed fresh pineapple (use a blender or food processor to make the puree)

Finely chopped zest (colored peel only) of ½ orange

½ cup dried cherries or cranberries

1 tablespoon Worcestershire sauce

Salt if needed

1. Heat the oven to 275 degrees. Set the ham in a foil-lined roasting pan or on a heavy baking sheet. Trim off the rind of the ham, leaving a ¼-inch covering of fat. Score the ham in two opposite directions at 1-inch intervals, cutting through the fat and about ¼ inch into the meat. (I like to score it on diagonals, creating a diamond pattern on the ham.)

2. With a brush, liberally baste the ham with *1 cup* of the salsa. Bake for 1½ hours.

3. With a brush, baste the ham with about *2 tablespoons* of the oil. Holding a small medium-mesh strainer over the ham, pour in the sugar and shake the strainer all over the ham to evenly coat it with sugar. Light a small blowtorch and, holding it about 3 inches from the surface of the ham, slowly wave it evenly over the whole surface to melt the sugar (it'll look crusty and slightly caramelized).

4. Return the ham to the oven and bake for about 1 hour more, until a meat or instant-read thermometer inserted into a thick part away from the bone registers about 140 degrees.

5. While the ham is baking, prepare the sauce: In a medium-size saucepan, heat the remaining *1 tablespoon* oil over medium. Add the onion and cook, stirring regularly, until richly browned, about 8 minutes. Add the remaining 2 *cups* salsa, the pineapple, orange zest, cherries or cranberries and Worcestershire. Simmer, stirring often, until reduced to the consistency of the original salsa, about 20 minutes. Cool to room temperature, then taste and season with a little salt if you think it needs it.

6. When the ham is ready, set it on a cutting board (a nice-looking wooden carving board is ideal here) and use a sharp, thin-bladed slicing knife (or an electric knife if you have one) to cut thin slices; you can serve it directly from the cutting board. Or for a more formal presentation, slice the ham and lay the slices, slightly overlapping, on a large serving platter. Serve the salsa in a decorative bowl for your guests to spoon on to their liking.

Guajillo-Spiked Shellfish Soup

Makes 12 cups, serving 6 as a main dish

If you've ever eaten a spicy Asian or Mediterranean fish soup, you'll know the satisfaction this page can bring. Infusing the broth with the rich, spicy tang of guajillo salsa adds marvelous depth of flavor to a rather simple preparation. In fact, getting different kinds of good shellfish may be the only challenge. (If some of them aren't available, just make the soup with all clams, all mussels or all shrimp.) When you set the bowls before your lucky guests, along with a basket of crusty bread, they'll love it.

3 cups Roasty Red Guajillo Salsa (page 33)
1 tablespoon vegetable or olive oil
10 cups rich-tasting chicken or fish broth
8 small (about 1 pound) red-skinned potatoes, scrubbed, each cut into 8 wedges
1 cup chopped fresh cilantro
1 pound (about 2 dozen) tightly closed fresh clams, scrubbed
1 pound (about 3 dozen) tightly closed fresh mussels, scrubbed and debearded

1 pound medium-large (about 24) shrimp, peeled (you can leave the final joint and tail on for nice looks if you like) and deveined
1 small white onion, finely chopped
Salt, about ½ teaspoon for salted broth, 1 teaspoon for unsalted broth
A couple of limes, cut into wedges, for garnish
Crushed red pepper flakes (optional)

1. Puree the salsa in a blender and press through a medium-mesh strainer into a bowl. Heat the oil in a large soup pot over medium. Add the salsa and cook, stirring frequently, until cooked down to the consistency of tomato paste, 3 to 5 minutes. Stir in the broth and potatoes. Partially cover and simmer over medium-low heat until the potatoes are just tender, about 10 minutes.

2. Raise the heat to medium-high. Stir in *half* of the cilantro, the clams and mussels; re-cover and cook until the shellfish open, about 5 minutes (if the liquid begins to boil too vigorously, reduce the heat a little). Stir in the shrimp, re-cover, remove from the heat and let stand for 3 minutes. While you're waiting, scoop the onion into a small strainer, rinse under cold water, shake off the excess liquid and mix (still in the strainer) with the remaining ½ *cup* cilantro. Taste the shellfish stew and season with salt. Ladle it into warm bowls and top each serving with a generous sprinkling of the onion and cilantro. Serve with wedges of lime, dipped in crushed red pepper flakes if you like, for each guest to squeeze in.

Red Chile Rice with Shrimp and Bacon

Serves 6

I think you'll understand why I love rice dishes so much when you taste this one—the robust, complex red-chile flavor is infused into plump rice grains (you definitely get the best texture from medium-grain rice), which are nestled around perfectly cooked shrimp. Not only could I eat this dish day after day, but it's one that always comes to mind as an easily likable one-pot main dish for casual entertaining. Add a salad and you've got all you need.

To serve Red Chile Rice on a buffet, you may want to choose small shrimp and peel them completely (taking off the final joint and tail) for the convenience of your guests. Don't forget to mix everything well before serving, since bits of salsa and green onions rise to the top during baking.

4 thick slices smoked bacon, cut into
   ½-inch pieces
2 cups rice, preferably medium grain
2 cups Mellow Red Chile Salsa (page 30)
1½ cups hot rich-tasting chicken broth or
   hot water
½ teaspoon salt

4 green onions, sliced crosswise ¼ inch
   thick
1 pound medium-large (about 24) shrimp,
   peeled and deveined
½ cup chopped fresh cilantro

1. Heat the oven to 350 degrees. In a 3-quart ovenproof saucepan, cook the bacon over medium heat, stirring, until crispy and brown, about 5 minutes. Remove with a slotted spoon, leaving behind the fat (you'll need a generous tablespoon to fry the rice). Set the crisp bacon aside. Add the rice to the pan and cook, stirring, until lightly browned, about 5 minutes.

2. Add the salsa and stir for 1 minute, then add the broth, salt and green onions. Bring to a boil, stir once, cover tightly and bake for 25 minutes. Remove from the oven.

3. Uncover and lay the shrimp on top of the rice mixture; re-cover and bake until the shrimp is opaque, 7 to 10 minutes. Sprinkle with the cilantro and crispy bacon, mix everything thoroughly with a fork and serve.

Seared Sea Scallops with Jalapeño Cream

Serves 4

If I were to serve this luscious sauce over fettuccine, I'd call it New World Alfredo. It's just that good, and in most of the same ways—though the sauce described in this recipe has added sparkle from the salsa's roasted tomatoes, garlic and jalapeños. Scallops make an elegant presentation in this easy dish, but shrimp would be equally delicious; if that's your choice, cook them for a slightly shorter time than you do scallops.

16 large sea scallops (the bigger, the better—about 1¼ pounds total), tough opaque "foot" on the side of each scallop pulled off
2 tablespoons fresh lime juice
About ¼ teaspoon salt, plus more for sprinkling on the scallops
Freshly ground black pepper

1½ tablespoons olive oil
1½ cups Roasted Jalapeño-Tomato Salsa (page 23), or for a spicier dish, use the habanero variation
½ cup heavy (whipping) cream or crème fraîche
⅓ cup chopped fresh cilantro or parsley

1. Rinse the scallops and toss them in a large bowl with the lime juice and a liberal sprinkling of salt and pepper. Cover and refrigerate 1 to 2 hours. Remove from marinade and pat dry.

2. Heat the oil in a large heavy skillet (my favorite choices are well-seasoned cast iron and non-stick) over medium-high. Lay in the scallops. If you're not able to fit them in an uncrowded layer, sear the scallops in two batches. Fry until richly browned on one side, about 2 minutes, then turn them over with tongs or a spatula and sear the other side for 1 to 2 minutes more. Scallops are done to my taste when they're still a little translucent in the middle. Remove them to a warm plate and pour off all the oil left in the pan.

3. Return the pan to the heat and add the salsa. Stir for a couple of minutes as the salsa boils down, thickens and darkens. Reduce the heat to medium-low, stir in the cream and, when it is warm, taste and season with salt. Ladle a portion of sauce onto each of 4 warm dinner plates, then arrange the scallops on top. Sprinkle each plate liberally with cilantro or parsley and they're ready to carry to the table.

Green Chile Crab Cakes

Makes 8 cakes, serving 4 as a main dish

Though crab cakes have been celebrated by North American cooks from Portland, Maine, to Portland, Oregon, tortitas de jaiba, as Veracruz cooks would call them, remain a little-known regional Mexican specialty. These are spiced up with Roasted Tomatillo Salsa, with more salsa stirred into mayonnaise for a delicious sauce. Lump crab is beautiful and expensive; shredded claw meat is flavorful; frozen crab is usually watery.

1 cup Roasted Tomatillo Salsa (page 28)
1 large egg
¾ cup plus 2 tablespoons mayonnaise
1 cup fresh bread crumbs
1 pound fresh crabmeat, picked over carefully to remove any stray bits of shell

½ cup chopped fresh cilantro
½ teaspoon salt, plus a little for the sauce
2 tablespoons olive or vegetable oil
1 lime, cut into 8 wedges

1. Pour the salsa into a medium-fine strainer set over a bowl and press on it lightly to extract most of the liquid. Transfer three-quarters of the salsa's solids to a medium-size bowl, then stir in the egg, 2 *tablespoons* of the mayonnaise, the bread crumbs, the crab, *half* of the cilantro and the salt. Form the mixture into 8 patties, each ½ inch thick. Lay them on a small tray covered with plastic wrap, and if time, freeze for 30 minutes to firm the cakes.

2. In a small bowl, combine the remaining salsa solids with the remaining *1 cup* mayonnaise and the remaining *¼ cup* cilantro. Stir in enough of the salsa "liquid" to make your sauce drizzleable but still thickish. Season with salt.

3. In a large skillet (nonstick works well here), heat the oil over medium. Lay the cakes in the hot oil in a single uncrowded layer and fry until crispy and browned on one side, about 3 minutes. Carefully flip the cakes over with a spatula and brown the other side, about 2 minutes more.

4. Arrange 2 cakes on each serving plate, drizzle with the sauce, and you're ready to enjoy them with your guests. Pass the lime wedges for squeezing on.

Red-Glazed Whole Fish

· · · · ·

Serves 4 generously

There's no dish with more rustic elegance—and adventure for most American cooks—than whole roast fish. And because of its succulence, any cook or eater who loves flavor and texture should know about fish roasted on the bone. Fillets can seem dry and tasteless by comparison.

I suggest you prepare a 1- to 1¼-pound fish for each guest. If they're not experienced at eating fish off the bone, instruct them as follows: Slice across the width of the fish just on the other side of the head, down to the bone. Then proceeding down the backbone (the part that would be at the top when the fish is swimming), work your fork and knife up under the flesh (staying close to that horizontal backbone). When your guests reach the ribs (they'll find them on the side opposite the top of the backbone), they'll have to go carefully, since the small pin bones connected to the ribs can be a little hard to see. Rather than roasting the fish with head and tail intact, you can also "pan dress" them by cutting off the heads and tails before marinating them.

4 1- to 1-¼-pound whole dressed snappers, pompanos, bass or other similar fish (catfish will work, though it wouldn't be my first choice; trout and small flounders are very delicate for this preparation)

2 tablespoons olive oil, plus a little more for oiling the baking dishes and onions

2½ cups Mellow Red Chile Salsa (page 30)

¼ cup good-quality orange marmalade

2 tablespoons fresh lime juice

4 green onions

1 teaspoon finely chopped orange zest (colored peel only)

I. With kitchen shears, trim the fins from the top, bottom and sides of the fish, then snip out the red gills (you can ask your fishmonger to do this for you). Make 3 diagonal slashes, cutting clear down to the backbone, across both sides of each fish, angling the slashes toward the tail. Lightly oil two 13 x 9-inch baking dishes (or similar pans—roasting pans work well here) and lay the fish in them.

2. Measure 1½ *cups* of the salsa into a blender or food processor and add the marmalade and lime juice. Process to a smooth puree, then press through a medium-mesh strainer into a small bowl. Brush half the salsa mixture over both sides of the fish, cover with plastic wrap and refrigerate for an hour or as long as 4 hours. (Refrigerate the remaining salsa mixture.)

3. Heat the oven to 400 degrees. Mix 2 tablespoons olive oil with the remaining salsa mixture and brush half of that over the fish. Brush the green onions with a little oil and lay them in the roasting pans alongside the fish. Set the pans in the oven and roast for 10 minutes. Brush with the remaining salsa mixture and roast for about 10 minutes longer, just until the fish is beautifully glazed and cooked through—the fish will flake away from the bone (test it with the point of a small knife at the thickest part, near where the flesh meets the head).

4. With a large metal spatula, transfer the fish to warm serving plates. Chop the roasted green onions into little bits and stir them into the remaining *1 cup* salsa along with the orange zest. Spoon a ribbon of salsa over the fish and carry proudly to the table.

Poblano-Baked Fish Fillets

Serves 4

Really fresh fish baked on slices of Yukon gold potatoes and blanketed with roasted tomatoes and poblanos is just about the tastiest, leanest meal you can make. If you'd like to dress up the dish for an elegant affair, arrange a quarter of the potatoes (after they've been cooked) in each of 4 individual casserole dishes (I like to use little earthenware cazuelas I brought back from Mexico). Top the potatoes with a fish fillet and a quarter of the salsa, then bake as I've described in the recipe. Set the hot, aromatic casseroles on heatproof plates in front of each guest.

4 medium-large (about 1½ pounds total) Yukon gold or baking potatoes, scrubbed and sliced ¼ inch thick
1 tablespoon olive oil
½ teaspoon salt
Four 5- to 6-ounce boneless, skinless fish fillets (choose a fish that's still moist when it's cooked through, such as snapper, grouper, halibut, mahi-mahi or sea bass)

2 cups Roasted Poblano-Tomato Salsa (page 26)
A couple of tablespoons chopped fresh cilantro, for garnish

I. Heat the oven to 400 degrees. In a 13 x 9-inch baking dish, mix the potatoes with the oil and salt to evenly coat. Cover with plastic wrap, turning back one corner of the plastic to allow steam to escape. Microwave on high, turning the dish occasionally, until the potatoes are almost tender, about 10 minutes. (If you don't have a microwave oven at your disposal, simply blanch the potatoes in heavily salted boiling water until nearly tender, drain thoroughly, mix with the oil to coat and spread in a lightly oiled 13 x 9-inch baking dish.)

2. Arrange the fish fillets over the potatoes without allowing them to touch each other. Spoon the salsa over the fillets and potatoes. Bake until the fish is just done (it will flake under firm pressure—use the back of a fork to press on it), 10 to 15 minutes. Sprinkle with the cilantro and carry to the table to dish up for your friends or family.

DESSERTS AND DRINKS

FRONTERA'S CHOCOLATE PECAN PIE BARS • TEXAS
SHEET CAKE • MEXICAN CHOCOLATE ICE-CREAM CONES •
PALETAS MEXICANAS (MEXICAN FRUIT POPS) • SANGRITA—
TRADITIONAL SPICY TEQUILA CHASER •
HONEST-TO-GOODNESS MARGARITAS FOR A CROWD

Frontera's Chocolate Pecan Pie Bars

Makes 24 bars

Many yearn for the sticky specialness of the typical Southern pecan pie (I grew up on it), but my tastes have changed. I want my nuts and syrup studded with bittersweet chocolate now, so that's what I designed for our house specialty dessert at Frontera Grill a dozen years ago. Here I've turned the same approach into bars, simplifying my original pie recipe and giving it a form that's right for a buffet or party. Rather than pastry, I've made an easy crust of bread crumbs and crunchy Mexican chocolate, then filled it with nuts and chocolate held together with just a bit of stickiness. You may find it easiest to line your pan with a carefully flattened piece of heavy-duty foil to help lift the bars out. Chilling the baked bars will make them easier to cut.

2½ cups (about 10 ounces) pecan halves

1 cup (about 6 ounces) finely chopped Mexican chocolate (such as the widely available Ibarra brand)

6 ounces (6 to 8 slices) fresh white bread, preferably firm sandwich-style bread (like Pepperidge Farm), broken into large pieces

1 cup (8 ounces) melted butter, plus extra for coating the pan

A generous ¾ teaspoon salt

5 ounces semisweet or bittersweet chocolate, chopped into pieces not larger than ¼ inch

3 tablespoons all-purpose flour

4 large eggs

1 cup firmly packed dark brown sugar

1 cup corn syrup, preferably dark (or use a mixture of corn syrup and molasses, sorghum, Steens cane syrup or most any of the other rich-flavored syrups that are on the market)

2 teaspoons pure vanilla extract

Powdered sugar, for garnish

1. Heat the oven to 325 degrees. Spread the pecans on a baking sheet and bake until browned and toasty smelling, about 10 minutes. Let cool, then scoop into a food processor and coarsely chop by quickly pulsing the machine on and off. Remove about 1½ cups of the nuts and put them in a large bowl to use in the filling. Add *half* of the Mexican chocolate to the nuts in the food processor and pulse the machine to mix them. Add the bread and process until everything is fairly fine crumbs. Add ⅓ *cup* of the melted butter and ¼ *teaspoon* of the salt; process just to moisten everything. (Lacking a food processor, you can chop each item separately with any other appliance or gadget you deem appropriate, then combine them in a bowl with the melted butter and salt.) Liberally butter a 13 x 9-inch baking pan, then evenly pat in the crumb-crust mixture. Refrigerate while you make the filling.

2. Add the remaining ½ *cup* Mexican chocolate, the semisweet chocolate and flour to the bowl with the reserved pecans. In the food processor (you don't even need to clean it), mix the eggs and sugar until well combined. Add the corn syrup and pulse a couple of times. Add the remaining ⅔ *cup* melted butter, the remaining ½ *teaspoon* salt and the vanilla; process to combine thoroughly. Add to the filling mixture, stir well and scrape everything into the crust-lined pan.

3. Bake for 40 to 50 minutes or until the bars have pulled away slightly from the side of the pan. Let cool to room temperature. Cut into 2-inch squares, dust with powdered sugar and arrange the bars on an attractive serving platter.

Texas Sheet Cake

Makes twenty-four 3-inch squares

This was my dessert growing up in Oklahoma, probably because I couldn't stay away from the chocolatey ooze created by spreading warm chocolate frosting on warm chocolate cake. I had mastered its preparation by age ten (it's very easy) and found myself regularly pressed into duty to make it. After years in professional kitchens, I've modified the recipe slightly—I've made it a little less sweet and substituted tenderizing powdered sugar for granulated—to keep up with the times, you could say. The "sheet" in the title refers to the pan size. Larger and deeper than a standard jelly-roll pan, a sheet pan (in this case a half-sheet pan) is a typical baking sheet in restaurants; it's very sturdy, not very expensive and available at restaurant supply houses, specialty cookware shops and even some warehouse clubs. Feel free to finish the cake a day or so ahead; well wrapped and refrigerated, it keeps nicely. If the microwave seems a convenient option, use it to make the frosting.

FOR THE CAKE:

10 tablespoons (5 ounces) unsalted butter, cut into ½-inch slices

1⅓ cups water

⅔ cup vegetable oil

2 large eggs

1 large egg yolk

⅔ cup buttermilk

1½ teaspoons pure vanilla extract

3 cups (13 ounces) all-purpose flour

1¼ pounds (about 5⅔ cups sifted) powdered sugar

½ cup (2 ounces) unsweetened cocoa powder

1½ teaspoons baking soda

½ teaspoon salt

FOR THE FROSTING AND TOPPING:

8 tablespoons (4 ounces) unsalted butter, cut into ½-inch slices

6 tablespoons milk

1 teaspoon pure vanilla extract

1 pound (about 4½ sifted cups) powdered sugar

⅓ cup (1½ ounces) unsweetened cocoa powder

2 cups (about 8 ounces) chopped pecans, toasted if you like

1. Heat the oven to 350 degrees. Butter and flour a 18 x 13-inch half-sheet pan (this pan is larger than the 15 x 10-inch "jelly-roll" pan, but it's the standard pan for this "sheet" cake).

2. For the cake, combine the butter, water and oil in a small saucepan. Stir over medium heat until the butter melts, then remove from the heat.

3. In a small bowl, beat together the eggs, egg yolk, buttermilk and vanilla.

4. Into a large bowl, sift together the flour, powdered sugar, cocoa, baking soda and salt. Add the butter mixture and beat thoroughly with a wooden spoon until everything is well combined. Add the egg mixture and beat for a couple of minutes (all this beating can be done with a stand or portable mixer if that suits you).

5. Pour the batter into the prepared pan and bake for 20 to 25 minutes, until the center springs back when lightly touched.

6. While the cake is baking, prepare the frosting (don't start before the cake goes into the oven because the frosting needs to be warm when it goes onto the warm cake). In a small saucepan, combine the butter and milk. Stir over medium heat until the butter melts, then remove from the heat and stir in the vanilla. Into a large bowl, sift together the powdered sugar and cocoa. Pour in the warm milk mixture and stir to combine.

7. When the cake comes out of the oven, let it stand 3 or 4 minutes, then dollop the frosting over it. Use a spatula to gently spread it evenly over the cake. Sprinkle with the pecans and let cool completely. I like to cut the cake into 3-inch squares, sprinkle them lightly with a little extra powdered sugar and serve them with ice cream.

Mexican Chocolate Ice-Cream Cones

Makes 12 cones

Okay, I may be out on a limb here, but I'm sure there are a lot of you who love puttering in the kitchen as much as I do. This is your recipe, since everyone else will go out and buy cones, fill them with ice cream and sprinkle on the crunchy Mexican chocolate instead of baking it in the cones. There's nothing really tricky about making these ice-cream cones (yes, you're reading that right: I've asked you to buy a box of cones so you can use a couple as molds). The batter is the same one used for making the classic French cookie tuile, which is wrapped around a rolling pin when it comes out of the oven. You bake these the same way, a couple at a time, then while they're still hot, you shape them into cones. If cone shapes prove a challenge, make little "cups" by draping the warm rounds over the backs of custard cups, or simply leave them flat and make ice-cream sandwiches. They crisp as they cool but will soften again with humidity in the air, so it is best to serve them within a few hours of making.

3 large egg whites

½ cup sugar

⅓ cup (2 ounces) pulverized Mexican chocolate (such as the Ibarra brand; pulse the roughly chopped chocolate in a food processor to pulverize it)

6 tablespoons (3 ounces) unsalted butter, at room temperature

1 teaspoon pure vanilla extract

¾ cup all-purpose flour

⅔ cup sliced almonds, toasted

3 conical waffle ice-cream cones, to use as molds

1 quart ice cream (chocolate-almond, vanilla bean or practically any fruit ice cream will be wonderful here)

About 1 cup just about any diced fresh fruit (strawberries, mango, papaya, peaches—even whole raspberries or small blackberries)

1. Heat the oven to 325 degrees. Pour about 1 inch water into a medium-size saucepan, set over medium heat and bring to a simmer. In a metal mixing bowl, thoroughly combine the egg whites, sugar and Mexican chocolate, set over the simmering water and stir until just warm to the touch. Remove from the heat, add the butter and stir until completely incorporated. Mix in the vanilla and flour.

2. Line a large baking sheet with a piece of parchment paper. Use a small spreading spatula to smear a scant 2 tablespoons batter in an even 5-inch round on the paper. (It is helpful to draw a 5-inch circle on the parchment first. Three circles fit nicely on a baking sheet.) Repeat with a second and third round, spacing them evenly from each other and from the sides. Sprinkle each one with a scant tablespoon of almonds. Bake for about 15 minutes, until the edges are a rich golden brown. While these are baking, set out the 3 waffle cones to use as molds.

3. Set the hot baking sheet near the cone molds, and working quickly, use a thin metal spatula to slide under one of the rounds, carefully lift it off the sheet and form it into a cone around one of the molds. Do the same with the other two rounds. If the rounds have baked too long, they'll crisp so quickly that forming cones will be nearly impossible. If they've simply cooled off and crisped right on the sheet, return the sheet to the oven for a couple of minutes and continue. When your homemade cones are cool, gently dislodge them from the molds. Bake and form the remaining cones in the same manner.

4. When you're ready to serve your hand-crafted ice-cream cones, scoop a ball of ice cream into a cone, spoon on some of the fruit and hand it to a guest. If the bottom of the cone isn't completely closed, you can drop in an M&M to plug it up. Keep filling cones until everyone is served.

*P*aletas Mexicanas (Mexican Fruit Pops)

Makes eight
2-ounce pops

On warm days all throughout our neighborhood, I can hear the jingling bells of the paletero *signaling to all of us the arrival of his sweet frozen fruit on sticks—from guanabana and papaya to coconut and tamarind. Given that there are several types of molds available in cookware stores and discount department stores, you'll be able to make these frozen fruit pops easily at home. Lacking the molds, partially freeze fruit purees in small paper cups, then stand wooden sticks (available at craft stores) in them (for added support lay a piece of cardboard over them with holes to keep the sticks upright). Frozen tropical fruit purees are available in Mexican grocery stores, but they're even better made from fresh fruit.*

Scant 2 cups coarsely pureed, peeled and pitted fruit (for really thick purees, like mango, you'll probably want to use 1½ cups fruit and ½ cup water; with looser purees, I wouldn't add any water)

1 to 4 tablespoons sugar—superfine sugar works best here (buy it or make it by grinding granulated sugar in a food processor for several minutes)
½ to 2 tablespoons fresh lime juice

1. In a medium-size bowl or a 1-quart measuring cup with a pour spout, combine the pureed fruit with the minimum quantities of sugar and lime. Taste and determine what your fruit needs. Remember, when the mixture is frozen, flavors will be slightly muted; go for slightly sweeter and slightly tarter than you'd normally like. Stir the mixture until the sugar has dissolved completely. Fill your molds, leaving about ¼-inch headspace to allow for expansion, set the lids in place and insert the sticks through the holes, leaving 1½ to 2 inches exposed.

2. Freeze until firmly set (this should take a couple of hours, though feel free to make them several days ahead if that's more convenient). To remove the pops, first remove the lids, then squeeze the sides of the molds, twisting them slightly, to dislodge the pop. (If necessary, rinse the molds quickly under hot water first.) These look festive and fun set out for your friends in a chilled bowl, all the sticks poking up.

Sangrita—traditional spicy tequila chaser

· · · ·

Makes about 2 3/4 cups, enough for 10 "chasers" or more

Though the absolutely highest quality tequilas are best enjoyed in snifters without even the thought of accompaniment beyond salted nuts or olives, many tequila drinkers are used to thinking of tequila with the lime-and-salt slam or the less rambunctious bottled sangrita chaser. While the latter is a little like bottled V-8 with lime and chile added, the original recipe doesn't call for tomato at all. I'm including a version of the original here, from the Comida Jaliscience *magazine published by Mexico Desconocido. I love to drink a little after a taste of full-flavored silver tequila (what's called* blanco *in Mexico) such as Chinaco from Tamaulipas or Corralejo from Michoacan.*

2 cups fresh orange juice
1/4 cup fresh lime juice, plus a little more if needed
2 tablespoons grenadine syrup
1/4 cup Mexican red hot sauce, such as La Valentina, Búfalo or Tamazula

2 tablespoons grated white onion, rinsed well
1 teaspoon Worcestershire
1/2 teaspoon salt

Stir together all ingredients, preferably in a glass or ceramic pitcher. I prefer to refrigerate the sangrita until very cold, but I always serve it the same day it's made, poured into tall shot glasses (called *caballitos* in Mexico)—the same ones used for tequila.

Honest-to-Goodness Margaritas for a Crowd

Makes 20 to 24 old-fashioned margaritas

In the age of the 32-ounce Big Gulp, a small drink may not seem fashionable. But quantity is not always related to quality, as is attested by most mammoth margaritas, laced as they are with artificially flavored sweet-and-sour mix. This margarita is the real thing—purity and refreshing freshness that's strained into martini glasses after a vigorous rumble with ice cubes in a cocktail shaker. Just before your guests arrive, combine the tequila, orange liqueur and lime juice in a pitcher, and you'll be poised for the shaking to begin. Though we gave an "equal part" recipe for the three main ingredients in our Top-of-the-Line Margarita in Rick Bayless's Mexican Kitchen, these proportions focus a bit more on the flavor of the good tequila. And it's silver (unaged) tequila here, the freshest and most agave-flavored of the tequilas. Reposado (six-month-old) tequila is a little softer and without the bright freshness of a silver, while the añejo (aged) tequila is moving toward the flavor of an aged brandy—and I personally don't think that's what margarita flavor is all about.

1 750-milliliter bottle silver tequila (in this margarita, the better the tequila, the better the drink; try Herradura, El Tesoro, El Viejito, Patron or practically any one of the 100 percent agave tequilas that are available)

1 to 2 cups (⅓ to ⅔ of a 750-milliliter bottle) Cointreau or Triple Sec

1 cup freshly squeezed lime juice, plus several tablespoons extra for rimming the glasses

Several tablespoons coarse kosher-type salt, for rimming the glasses

About 1 gallon ice cubes

1. Just before serving, in a half-gallon pitcher combine the tequila, the minimum amount of Cointreau or Triple Sec and the lime juice. Taste and add more orange liqueur if you think your margaritas need more sweet oranginess to balance the other flavors. Remember, you're tasting it warm and undiluted; when chilled and diluted, the flavors will be mellower and the lime's tartness will be more attractive (tangy warm champagne is not nearly as inviting as it is ice-cold).

2. Pour several tablespoons of lime juice onto one small plate and several tablespoons coarse salt onto another. Have martini glasses at hand (for an extra special touch, you can chill them); I like the 5-ounce size, since that size drink will stay cold from first sip to last.

3. As your guests ask for their margaritas, invert a glass into the plate with the lime juice to moisten the rim, then lightly dip it into the plate with the salt. For each drink measure 2 ounces (¼ cup) of the margarita mixture into a cocktail shaker (I can do 3 drinks at a time comfortably in mine). If you have a 2-ounce ladle that you can keep in the pitcher, measuring goes much faster. Add ice cubes (I put in 5 cubes for 1, 8 for 2, and 10 for 3). Secure the lid and top and shake vigorously for 10 to 15 seconds. Strain into the salt-crusted glasses and hand off to the lucky recipients.

MAIL-ORDER SOURCES

Alltrista Consumer Products Co.
P.O. Box 2729
Muncie, IN 47307
800-340-2240

Canning supplies,
home canning guide

Chile Today Hot Tamale
2D Great Meadow Lane
East Hanover, NJ 07936
800-468-7377
www.chiletoday.com

Dried chiles, canned chipotles

The CMC Company
P.O. Box 322
Avalon, NJ 08202
800-CMC-2780

Dried chiles, canned chipotles,
masa harina, Mexican oregano,
Mexican chocolate

Dean & Deluca
Catalogue Department
2526 E. 36th St.
North Circle
Wichita, KS 67219
800-221-7714

Dried chiles, *masa harina*

Frontera Foods, Inc.
449 N. Clark St.
Chicago, IL 60610
800-509-4441

Salsas, hot sauces

The King Arthur Flour
Baker's Catalogue
P.O. Box 876
Norwich, VT 05055-0876
800-827-6836

Mexican vanilla, *masa harina,*
half-sheet pan, oil mister

New York Cake and Baking
Distributor
56 W. 22nd St.
New York, NY 10010
800-94-cake-9

Half-sheet pans, fruit pop molds
and sticks

Penzey's Spices
P.O. Box 933
Muskego, WI 53150
414-679-7207

Dried chiles, Mexican oregano

The Spice House
1941 Central St.
Evanston, IL 60201
847-328-3711
www.thespicehouse.com

Dried chiles, Mexican oregano,
Mexican vanilla

INDEX

A

asparagus, roasted, tomatillo-baked chicken breasts with, 85

avocado(s):
crispy *masa* boat snacks with black beans, salsa, Mexican cheese and, 46–47
in great tortilla soup, 52
shrimp *salpicón* salad with potatoes, chipotle and, 54–55
in tangy green guacamole, 40
tiny tostadas of smoky chicken *tinga* with aged cheese and, 43

B

bacon:
red chile rice with shrimp and, 105
tomatillo-braised pork loin with herby white beans and, 98–99

bars, Frontera's chocolate pecan pie, 112–13

bean(s), black:
and chorizo chili, 96
crispy *masa* boat snacks with salsa, avocado, Mexican cheese and, 46–47
in spicy vegetable "stew," 73
toasty *fideos* (vermicelli) with roasted tomato, chard and, 74–75

beans, garbanzo, in spicy vegetable "stew," 73

beans, green, in spicy vegetable "stew," 73

beans, white, herby, tomatillo-braised pork loin with bacon and, 98–99

beef:
brisket, robust, with red chile and winter vegetables, 92–93
peppery pan-seared steaks with smoky *crema* and blue cheese, 94–95
tips, spicy jalapeño, 97

beets, in poblano-roasted vegetable salad with peppery watercress, 57

black bean(s):
and chorizo chili, 96
crispy *masa* boat snacks with salsa, avocado, Mexican cheese and, 46–47
in spicy vegetable "stew," 73
toasty *fideos* (vermicelli) with roasted tomato, chard and, 74–75

blue cheese, peppery pan-seared steaks with smoky *crema* and, 94–95

bread pudding, savory brunch, 70

breakfast enchiladas of scrambled eggs, woodland mushrooms and spicy roasted tomatoes, 68–69

brisket, robust beef, with red chile and winter vegetables, 92–93

brunch bread pudding, savory, 70

C

cake, Texas sheet, 114–15

carrots, in robust beef brisket with red chile and winter vegetables, 92–93

cascabel-chipotle salsa with roasted tomatoes and tomatillos, 36–38

casserole, tortilla (*chilaquiles*), with spinach, zucchini and aged cheese, 76–77

chard, toasty *fideos* (vermicelli) with roasted tomato, black beans and, 74–75

chayote(s):
in guajillo grilled vegetables, 60–61
in spicy vegetable "stew," 73

chayote(s) (*cont.*)
tangy lentil salad with spinach, cilantro and, 58–59

cheese:
blue, peppery pan-seared steaks with smoky *crema* and, 94–95
in breakfast enchiladas of scrambled eggs, woodland mushrooms, and spicy roasted tomatoes, 68–69
goat, salsa-baked, 41
in great tortilla soup, 52
layered tortilla "lasagna" with greens and, 80–81
Mexican, crispy *masa* boat snacks with black beans, salsa, avocado and, 46–47
in open-face quesadillas with mushrooms, olives, salsa and greens, 42
in scalloped potatoes with roasted tomatillos, serranos and cilantro, 64
in toasty *fideos* (vermicelli) with roasted tomato, black beans and chard, 74–75
today's macaroni and, —it's not just for kids, 72

cheese, aged:
chilaquiles (tortilla casserole) with spinach, zucchini and, 76–77
seared red-chile enchiladas with chicken and, 78–79
tiny tostadas of smoky chicken *tinga* with avocado and, 43

chicken:
breast, grilled, soft tacos of, with tangy green chile and grilled onions, 86–87
breasts, tomatillo-baked, with roasted asparagus, 85
chile-glazed roast, 84

chicken (*cont.*)
  seared red-chile enchiladas with
  aged cheese and, 78–79
  tinga, smoky, with avocado and
  aged cheese, tiny tostadas of, 43
chilaquiles (tortilla casserole)
  with spinach, zucchini and
  aged cheese, 76–77
chile(s):
  dried, 20–21
  fresh, 19–20
  glazed roast chicken, 84
  green, crab cakes, 107
  salsa, mellow red, with sweet
  garlic and roasted tomatoes,
  30–32
  tangy green, soft tacos of grilled
  chicken breast with grilled
  onions and, 86–87
  see also specific chiles
chili(ed):
  chorizo and black bean, 96
  pork empanadas, sweet-and-
  spicy, 44–45
chipotle:
  mashed potatoes, 63
  shrimp *salpicón* salad with potatoes, avocados and, 54–55
chipotle-cascabel salsa with
  roasted tomatoes and tomatillos, 36–38
  in chile-glazed roast chicken, 84
  in chipotle mashed potatoes, 63
  in layered tortilla "lasagna" with
  greens and cheese, 80–81
  in peppery pan-seared steaks
  with smoky *crema* and blue
  cheese, 94–95
  in savory brunch bread pudding,
  70
  in shrimp *salpicón* salad with
  potatoes, avocados and chipotle, 54–55
  in smoky glazed ham for a
  crowd, 102–3
  in spicy vegetable "stew," 73
  in tiny tostadas of smoky
  chicken *tinga* with avocado and
  aged cheese, 43

chips, microwave "baked," 49
chocolate:
  Mexican, ice-cream cones,
  116–17
  pecan pie bars, Frontera's,
  112–13
  in Texas sheet cake, 114–15
chorizo:
  and black bean chili, 96
  -potato omelet, open-face, with
  tomatillo salsa, 67
chowder, emerald corn, with
  roasted tomatillos and poblano,
  53
cilantro:
  fresh, roasted jalapeño-tomato
  salsa with, 23–25
  roasted tomatillo salsa with serranos, roasted onions and,
  28–29
  scalloped potatoes with roasted
  tomatillos, serranos and, 64
  tangy lentil salad with spinach,
  chayote and, 58–59
clams, in guajillo-spiked shellfish
  soup, 104
corn:
  chowder with roasted tomatillos
  and poblano, emerald, 53
  in layered tortilla "lasagna" with
  greens and cheese, 80–81
  Cornish hens, burnished, with
  roasted onions and sweet potatoes, 88–89
crab cakes, green chile, 107
cream, jalapeño, seared sea scallops with, 106
crema, smoky, peppery pan-
  seared steaks with blue cheese
  and, 94–95

D
desserts:
  Frontera's chocolate pecan pie
  bars, 112–13
  Mexican chocolate ice-cream
  cones, 116–17
  paletas mexicanas (Mexican fruit
  pops), 118

desserts (*cont.*)
  Texas sheet cake, 114–15
drinks:
  honest-to-goodness margaritas
  for a crowd, 120
  sangrita—traditional spicy
  tequila chaser, 119

E
eggplant:
  in guajillo grilled vegetables,
  60–61
  omelets, racy, with savory red
  chile, 66
eggs:
  open-face chorizo-potato omelet
  with tomatillo salsa, 67
  racy eggplant omelets with savory red chile, 66
  in savory brunch bread pudding,
  70
  scrambled, breakfast enchiladas
  of woodland mushrooms,
  spicy roasted tomatoes and,
  68–69
empanadas, sweet-and-spicy
  chilied pork, 44–45
enchiladas:
  of scrambled eggs, woodland
  mushrooms and spicy roasted
  tomatoes, breakfast, 68–69
  seared red-chile, with chicken
  and aged cheese, 78–79
equipment and techniques, 17–19
escabeche, red, shrimp in, 48

F
fennel, in poblano-roasted vegetable salad with peppery watercress, 57
fideos (vermicelli), toasty, with
  roasted tomato, black beans
  and chard, 74–75
fish and shellfish:
  fillets, poblano-baked, 110
  green chile crab cakes, 107
  guajillo-spiked shellfish soup, 104
  red chile rice with shrimp and
  bacon, 105

fish and shellfish *(cont.)*
  red-glazed whole, 108–9
  seared sea scallops with
    jalapeño cream, 106
  shrimp in red escabeche, 48
  shrimp *salpicón* salad with pota-
    toes, avocados and chipotle,
    54–55
Frontera's chocolate pecan pie
  bars, 112–13
fruit pops, Mexican *(paletas mexicanas)*, 118

G
garbanzo beans, in spicy vegetable "stew," 73
garlic, 21
  sweet, and roasted tomatoes,
    mellow red chile salsa with,
    30–32
  sweet, roasty red guajillo salsa
    with tangy tomatillos and,
    33–35
goat cheese, salsa-baked, 41
green beans, in spicy vegetable
  "stew," 73
green chile:
  crab cakes, 107
  tangy, soft tacos of grilled
    chicken breast with grilled
    onions and, 86–87
greens:
  layered tortilla "lasagna" with
    cheese and, 80–81
  open-face quesadillas with mush-
    rooms, olives, salsa and, 42
guacamole, tangy green, 40
guajillo:
  grilled vegetables, 60–61
  salsa, roasty red, with tangy
    tomatillos and sweet garlic,
    33–35
  -spiked shellfish soup, 104

H
habanero-tomato salsa, roasted, 25
ham, smoky glazed, for a crowd,
  102–3
herbs, fresh, 21

herby white beans and bacon,
  tomatillo-braised pork loin
  with, 98–99

I
ice-cream cones, Mexican chocolate, 116–17
ingredients, choice of, 19–21

J
jalapeño:
  beef tips, spicy, 97
  cream, seared sea scallops with,
    106
  -tomato salsa, roasted, with
    fresh cilantro, 23–25
jícama-red chile salad with orange and red onion, 56

L
lamb leg (or turkey breast), slow-
  grilled, with Mediterranean
  salsa, 90–91
"lasagna," layered tortilla, with
  greens and cheese, 80–81
lentil salad, tangy, with spinach,
  cilantro and chayote, 58–59

M
macaroni and cheese, today's—
  it's not just for kids, 72
mail-order sources, 122
main courses:
  egg, vegetable, pasta and tortilla,
    65–81
  poultry, meat and fish,
    83–110
margaritas for a crowd, honest-
  to-goodness, 120
masa boat snacks, crispy, with
  black beans, salsa, avocado
  and Mexican cheese, 46–47
mellow red chile salsa with sweet
  garlic and roasted tomatoes,
  30–32
  in burnished Cornish hens with
    roasted onions and sweet pota-
    toes, 88–89
  in great tortilla soup, 52

mellow red chile salsa *(cont.)*
  in racy eggplant omelets with
    savory red chile, 66
  red chile-jícama salad with or-
    ange and red onion, 56
  in red chile pasta, 71
  in red chile rice with shrimp and
    bacon, 105
  in red-glazed whole fish,
    108–9
  in robust beef brisket with red
    chile and winter vegetables,
    92–93
  in seared red-chile enchiladas
    with chicken and aged cheese,
    78–79
  in sweet-and-spicy chilied pork
    empanadas, 44–45
mushrooms:
  in layered tortilla "lasagna" with
    greens and cheese, 80–81
  open-face quesadillas with
    olives, salsa, greens and, 42
  woodland, breakfast enchiladas
    of scrambled eggs, spicy
    roasted tomatoes and, 68–69
mussels, in guajillo-spiked shellfish soup, 104
mustardy sweet onions, grilled-
  and-glazed pork tenderloin
  with, 100–101

N
New Mexico chiles, in mellow
  red chile salsa with sweet garlic
  and roasted tomatoes, 30–32

O
olives, open-face quesadillas with
  mushrooms, salsa, greens and,
  42
omelet(s):
  open-face chorizo-potato, with
    tomatillo salsa, 67
  racy eggplant, with savory red
    chile, 66
onion(s), 21
  green, in guajillo grilled vegeta-
    bles, 60–61